THE TITLE IX GUY

SEVERAL SHORT ESSAYS ON RAPE
CULTURE, MASCULINITY (THE GOOD
KIND & THE BAD KIND), & OTHER
THINGS WE SHOULD BE TALKING ABOUT
| SECOND EDITION

JAMES J. WILKERSON

PROSE & PROOF
PUBLISHING COMPANY | KY

Prose and Proof Publishing Company

Second Edition

CONTENTS

Dedication   1

1. Hello, Again   3

2. The Time I Got Banned for Writing About Fraternity   6
   Brothers Holding Each Other Accountable

3. Extracurricular Activities: The Fetishization of Female   15
   Defendants in Sexual Misconduct Cases

4. Yeezy Taught Me: Kanye West and the Characteristics of   25
   Abuse

5. Attorneys Say the Darndest Things   34

6. Please Don't Share These: A Revenge Porn Primer   41

7. Fruit of the Poisonous Tree: How Toxic Masculinity   54
   Produces Sexual Assault

8. The New New Nine: Title IX Changes Through Two   61
   Vastly Different Administrations

9. What I Learned About Sexual Assault Education in   78
   Higher Education from NASPA

10. Cosby, Kelly, and Racial Injustice in Sexual Assault   89
    Cases

11. Politicians Say the Darndest Things   97

12. How Bad Do You Want In?   103

13. Why Doesn't She Just Say No?   123

14. (Non-Consensual) Sex on the Beach: Bystander Theory   152

15. When We Cry   167

16. The Monster at My Law School   181

17. References   205

About the author   249

To Blair, Harrison, and Alex
I love y'all.

1

HELLO, AGAIN

When the first edition of this book was released in 2021, it accomplished exactly what it was designed to; it provided my advocacy a volley of credibility.

Some academic street cred, if you will.

In the same way a PhD stands on their dissertation, I now had my own volume of research to hold above my head. And that collection became a key that unlocked new doors. Now when I was booked to speak, universities could say they were presenting a best-selling author. With my Ted Talks and growing list of conference engagements, the book was one of the last pieces of the "expert in his field" puzzle I needed to assemble.

Around this time, I had also began teaching college courses. And it was through this teaching, I answered a question that my original publisher never could; how do we promote this book? When I realized I could select any book I wanted for my class texts, it was a no brainer to use *The Title IX Guy* to teach masculinity to my gender studies students at Indiana University Southeast. It made absolute sense to use the book to teach the double standard for female defendants in sex abuse cases to my law students at the University of Louisville. *The Title IX Guy* went from an independent release to an academic textbook and has educated numerous college students on various academic levels.

Not too shabby of a placement for my first release.

In early 2024, my publisher decided that she wanted to put the focus of her press on queer poetry and as such, we struck a deal which saw the publishing rights for my first two books return to me.

So now I had to find a new publisher.

The publishing process for my second book taught me I did not want to deal with the drama and politics of a traditional academic press. I shopped around to some other indies, but balked at the amount they wanted me to pay up front for publishing (especially because I was more than capable of editing and laying out a book myself).

I decided to pull the trigger on a long-held idea. I established my own publishing press. Being published was one of the biggest honors I ever received as a student and through my own independent academic press, I could share that same honor with new generations of students, minus the stuffiness and pretentiousness of your standard college journal. I was also taking control of my own platform, which would give me the freedom to experiment with manner of non-traditional publishing ideas.

In 2024, Prose and Proof Publishing Company was born.

And what better book to be the inaugural release, than the second edition of the book that started it all.

This edition of *The Title IX Guy* contains four brand new chapters. Nonphysical domestic violence is discussed through the lens of Kanye West in the chapter, "Yeezy Taught Me". Universities are taken to task for bungling sexual assault education in "What I Learned About Sexual Assault Education in Higher Education from NASPA". I dig into men's mental health in "When We Cry" (which was also the topic of my final TEDx Talk for Lake Superior State University). And for my fellow law nerds out there, I analyze the latest Title IX regulations in "The New New Nine: Title IX Changes Through Two Vastly Different Administrations". Alongside the correction of few typos my previous editor missed the first time around, the second edition adds new and relevant research to an already sturdy foundation.

As for dedications, this book goes out to all of my students; past, present, and future. In the words of the great Professor Sam Marcosson, you can't change the world, unless you know what you're trying to change.

Allow me to show you.

May 5, 2024
Kitchen Table, Louisville, KY

2

---·---

THE TIME I GOT BANNED FOR WRITING ABOUT FRATERNITY BROTHERS HOLDING EACH OTHER ACCOUNTABLE

S exual assault on the college campus; it's never not a problem, how-ever sometimes it's more publicized than not. While Bill Cosby has been connected to most of the more resent sexual assault chatter on the interwebs, college fraternities are also not without controversy.

The above stanza were the first words I ever wrote about the topic of sexual assault. The year was 2014 and I was preparing for my first year at the Brandeis School of Law. Despite being in my 30's, I was excited about my student status, knowing my third degree would be my final one. In addition to late nights in the law library, serving on the school's student government and grueling hour-long practices as a member of the mock trial team, I also served as a student writer on a college blog.

Knet Books is an online college textbook seller and host of the KnetBooks Blog. The blog features a variety of college centric topics ranging from dealing with the stress of higher education to managing college debt. While my articles on Christmas gift ideas and my affinity for hooded sweatshirts were typically well received, when I made a written plea for fraternity men to hold one another accountable for their sexual behavior, I had crossed the line. My article would never see the light of day; it was banned.

Hush, Hush

The biggest story to break in recent months was the alleged gang rape at the University of Virginia which resulted in administration bringing a halt to fraternity life through the fall semester. Also, in last semester's news was a fraternity at the University of Wisconsin- Milwaukee who, in September, came under investigation for allegedly marking female party-goers hands with a red X, giving them access to drugged alcoholic beverages. To close the year out, two co-eds at Brown University tested positive for the date rape drug GHB, which found its way into their drinks during a party hosted by one of the University's fraternities. Fraternities are finding themselves at the very dangerous intersection of Drinking Culture and Hook -Up Culture, with the collisions adding up.

It was not the quality of my article that got itself banned but, rather, its topic. My editor stated that an article about collegiate sexual assault might upset some of their readers. Although I was too shortsighted to see it at the time, my editor's comment was directly tied to the taboo nature of sexual assault conversations. There is no doubt that sexual assault is a difficult topic to discuss. Cases on sexual assault usually contain traumatic and personal details of violent acts that many consider "too sensitive" for everyday conversation.

Parents struggle with the topic when they teach their children about sex, as the conversation is usually limited to warnings of pregnancy or sexually transmitted diseases. This leaves children to receive the bulk of their sexual education from their friends and internet porn, neither of which typically focus on the laws of sexual misconduct. Even educators experience barriers that cause them to think twice about starting these conversations. Teachers have cited a lack of education on the topic as a reason to avoid it altogether. Some have even expressed the fear of being accused of sexual harassment themselves as a reason for not including the topic as a part of their lesson plan.

Sidestepping sexual assault education is not limited to the K-12 sector. In my second semester of law school, we began our unit on sex crimes with a memorable address from our professor who explained that while our class would be trudging through this unit, there are law schools around the country that were skipping over these crimes due to their taboo nature. Indeed, law students around the country have voiced their concerns with the way sex crimes are taught, leading to professors choosing to skip the topic altogether, rather than adjust their teaching method.

For some, other cultural beliefs such as religious values place a taboo on sex (consensual or otherwise) in normal conversation. Take the Islamic faith, for example, which considers Zina (sex outside of marriage) a sin. A Muslim writer for the website Parhlo would discover that her religion's views on sex would lead to accusations that her 2015 article "10 Surprising Health Benefits of Having Sex" crossed her boundaries as a Muslim. Psychological research has attempted to explain the taboo nature of sex talk by tying it to the idea that sex reminds humans of our animalistic nature, thus igniting fears about our own morality that may be in conflict with our religious beliefs.

For men, self-reflection also serves as a barrier to discussing sexual assault because having honest discussions about rape culture requires a level of uncomfortable self-evaluation. Thinking of sexual assault as an abstract crime that happens to (and is caused by) strangers we do not know is easy. When the conversation is personalized, however, it creates a high level of turmoil for the members of the community in question. For fraternity men, these discussions are a journey into the shadows and dark spots in their organizations that they may not be ready to take.

Teaching Fraternity Men

In 2001, I was riding high in the "life" category. I had pledged a top house and was being accompanied by one the most popular and beautiful girls from my high school graduating class to our pref night, which was a mini cruise on a steamboat. Also, along for the ride was a pretty cool girl from my dorm, let's call her Beth, who was the date of one of the older brothers in the chapter. As the night went along, I noticed that Beth had proceeded past "fun drunk" right into "needs to be helped back to the dorm drunk." I also noticed her date getting increasingly flirty, which was troubling considering the fact that Beth could barely keep her eyes open and head upright. At this point, I pointed out the situation to my date and we made it our mission to get Beth back to the dorm safely. As I got to know the brother in question, I eventually learned that he is a pretty good guy, and when we finally discussed what happened that night, he informed me that while he would not take advantage of a girl, he was glad that I intervened as it showed good character. While this situation worked out in the end, there are more people not intervening than are.

I knew I wanted to join a fraternity before I even knew what university I would attend. The movie Animal House did the trick on glamorizing the fraternity life and by the time I made it to the University of Louisville, I was quickly seeking out Greek Row and joining the most fun-loving group on campus at the time, Tau Kappa Epsilon. It would be those days of themed parties, football tailgates, and fraternizing with sororities, that would set the foundation for my eventual excursion into advocacy 15 years later.

Fraternities live in an environment that utilizes a reactive approach when it comes to sexual assault. The internet overflows with stories of fraternity suspensions and disbandings due to sexual misconduct. Chapters engaged in this type of behavior can anticipate university sanctions, unfavorable media coverage and punishments from their national fraternity office . While a reactionary culture is needed to ensure chapters are abiding by Title IX regulations, a strong proactive culture helps students avoid these issues in the first place.

Breaking down the taboo wall for fraternity men should start on their first day as a new member (also known as a pledge or candidate). New members go through a period of education, (also known as pledgeship,) before being granted full membership in Greek organizations. The education in this period usually focuses on fraternity history, bylaws, customs, and traditions. By the time a member makes it to the end of this period, they will be immersed in the customs all full members are expected to follow. This period is when members should engage in the sexual assault conversation, as teaching prevention along with other fraternity customs places consent, bystander intervention, and healthy sexual behavior in the chapter's set of core values and expectations. Chapters such as Sigma Phi Epsilon at the University of Northern Iowa and full fraternity systems like those at the University of Pennsylvania are among those that integrate sexual assault education in their new members programs.

As stated earlier, a barrier that fraternity men encounter when speaking about sexual assault prevention is self-reflection. Fraternity men report feeling like university-led education on sexual assault is more akin to a "stern lecture" rather than a conversation. Being automatically painted as "the bad guy" is often a turnoff for members, causing them to go on the defense and disconnect from the talk altogether. When I was formulating a way for me to use my platform as a fraternity alum to educate active members on the principle of consent, I spoke with my university's Greek advisor who told a story of one of the past sexual assault presentations the fraternities participated in. The university center for prevention and education, sent a student activist to speak to members of the IFC (short for Interfraternity Council, the governing body for the predominantly white fraternities on college campuses). The very first words from the speaker's mouth were "one in four of all of you are rapists. Let's talk about it."

Although the opening line may have been harsh, the information was rooted in research. The statistic of one in four undergraduate college women being sexually assaulted has been cited frequently. Despite the statistical backing of her statement, however, the message was lost due to the delivery. In this instance, the barrier of self-reflection was elevated because of the speaker's accusatory tone. Though she didn't know it, her lecture was over before it even began. After that incident, the Greek advisor told me, "The members of IFC told me never to send someone from that office again."

Unlike the well-meaning speaker above, educating fraternity members on sexual assault is an exercise of "giving medicine with a spoonful of sugar." A positive educational experience is one where we speak with fraternity men, rather than at them. Creating a space that brothers consider safe to speak in, sans judgement, is key to helping them over the hurdles that prevent them from conversing on this topic. Also, designing education that is relatable and realistic, leads brothers to think and converse honestly and critically about sexual assault.

When putting together my initial lectures on consent, I made sure that every example was a story from my time as an active fraternity member. I filled my presentations with the same stories I would tell pals at the campus bar, repurposing them as tales of consent rather that anecdotes of conquest. The result was a laid back, comfortable atmosphere where my audience was engaged by examples that are similar to what many of them go through on a regular basis. By using relatable examples, fraternity brothers were able to see how they themselves unconsciously partook in healthy sexual behavior. This approach also serves to demonstrate how easy the concept of consent truly is.

Continuing Education

Of course, not every member of a fraternity is a sexual predator. On the contrary, a majority of fraternity men will express their disdain for this sort of behavior and resent the fact that their membership in a Greek organization even associates them with these despicable acts. These men need to be agents of change in their chapters. They are the ones who must band together and not only speak against sexual assault, but act against it. When an email entitled "Luring Your Rape bait" is sent out to the entire chapter, these men mustn't be bystanders laughing with the herd. Rather, these men must risk being "uncool" in order to say these "jokes" aren't funny but destructive. Instead of turning a blind eye to the party guest who has clearly had one too many and can't even spell the word "consent" as she is being coaxed into a random bedroom, these men must interject. These men must be the voices of reason when their brothers are making plans to disrupt a "Take Back the Night" rally by throwing eggs and sex toys at their fellow students who are legitimately concerned about their safety on campus. Simply put, if the culture is to change, these men must be men; simply being bystanders will no longer do.

After having my article rejected, I realized that my voice may be meant for something greater than penning top 10 lists. I left Knet Books and settled into my first semester of law school. In the spring of 2016, I would create Greek Law as a public service group through the school's student government. Through Greek Law, I would get the opportunity to work with hundreds of fraternity men and sorority women throughout the states of Kentucky, Indiana, Ohio, and Alabama. When I graduated, I would take Greek Law with me, turning it into a 501(c)(3) non-profit organization. Eventually I would develop a high school and middle school curriculum, helping secondary schools start the discussion of healthy sexual behavior with their students. In 2020 I would parlay this work into a full-time position at Indiana University Southeast, as their deputy Title IX coordinator, a position that allows me to continue the conversation of sexual assault prevention with our fraternity men. It is this continuation of the conversation that is needed to move the needle.

During the same years when fraternity members have filled the ranks of sexual assault awareness groups like Indiana University's Men Against Rape and Sexual Assault (MARS), fraternities like Washington State University's Delta Upsilon were suspended for a sexual assault at a party. At the same time when fraternity members at Kansas University formed a task force to address sexual assault in their Greek community, more than half of the campus sexual assaults reported at San Diego State University involved fraternity members. In the semester I would first have the opportunity to lecture the entire new member class of fraternity men at Western Kentucky University, a Sigma Tau Gamma pledge would record his sexual assault of a classmate at Purdue University, 278 miles away. While it is important to acknowledge and applaud the work chapters are doing to flatten the curve of fraternity sexual assault, it is equally important to remember that there is still a lot of work that must be done.

Small things like speaking up when an inappropriate joke is made or intervening in a suspect situation at a party are actions that change an entire culture. To arrive at this culture shift, fraternities must make conversations on healthy sexual behavior common and casual. And given the fact that each new school year welcomes a new class of freshmen, these conversations must also be consistent.

The same goes for blogs and other internet outlets that produce information about college life for students. These outlets must not shy away from addressing sexual assault because, unfortunately, sexual assault is just as much a part of higher education as rooting for the home team or arguing with your freshman year roommate. In the words of Louisville criminal law professor Sam Marcosson, "the first step to changing the world is to know what we're changing."

In a perfect world, students wouldn't have to avoid taking a night class or be wary about walking from the library to their dorm after a late-night study session. In a perfect world, students could attend parties in the most carefree of manners, void of any worry of a drugged drink. However, until this perfect world comes to fruition, these men, these bystanders, may be all she has.

3

—·—

EXTRACURRICULAR ACTIVITIES: THE FETISHIZATION OF FEMALE DEFENDANTS IN SEXUAL MISCONDUCT CASES

The Comment Section

Patrick Newman was a teacher and assistant football coach at the prestigious Trinity High School, located in Louisville, Kentucky. In 2015, Newman was accused of trading sexually explicit photos and videos with several teenage boys, ranging from 13 to 17 years old. Newman pled guilty to several child pornography charges and in 2016 he was sentenced to 43 years imprisonment.

The Courier Journal, Louisville's city newspaper, reported the story on their Facebook page, garnering comments from readers. Regarding Newman, one male reader commented that "his sentence was minimal considering the damage he did to so many young boys and their families." Another commenter stated that Newman would get what he deserved in prison as "prisoners love child molesters." And yet another echoed Newman's punishment wasn't enough, stating the sentence "should be the death penalty."

Several years later, in the nearby city of Owensboro, Kentucky, Ramsey BethAnn Bearse made headlines of her own. On December

2018, Bearse was arrested for sending at least four topless photos to a 15-year-old male student of hers when she worked as a teacher at Andrew Jackson Middle School in Cross Lanes, West Virginia. Bearse pled guilty in December 2019 to one felony count of possession of material depicting minors in sexually explicit conduct. In July 2020, Bearse was sentenced to two years in prison as well as 10 years of supervised release and a lifetime registration as a sex offender.

Perhaps due to Bearse's status as a former Miss Kentucky, her story was widely reported. USA Today reported the story on its Facebook page, however the comments from male readers differed from the ones the Newman story received. One male reader commented "all young men appreciate some mature trim. It's a natural thing." Several male readers dubbed the student as "a lucky kid," while another called Bearse the "best teacher in the world." Several male commenters responded to Bearse's sexual crime by professing their "love for America." Many expressed their desire to see the pics. Others simply commented, "nice."

Society's Double Standard

Newman and Bearse's stories highlight a societal double standard when it comes to male and female teachers committing sex crimes. Newman's story shows that men understand sexual misconduct with underage pupils is morally and legally wrong. Bearse's story on the other hand, shows that same morality and legal understanding is easily set aside when the sexual offender is an attractive woman.

The Comedy Central animated series, South Park, perfectly addressed this double standard in the tenth episode of their tenth season entitled, "Miss Teacher Bangs a Boy." In the episode, a kindergarten teacher is having sexual relationship with one of her students. When the student's older brother, Kyle, reports the misconduct to the police, the officers mistakenly assume Kyle is referencing a male teacher having sex with a female student. As the officers spring into action, ready to arrest the teacher, Kyle clarifies that it is actually a female teacher having sex with a boy. Once the officers confirm that the teacher "isn't ugly," their attitudes instantly change, referring to the situation as "nice." An officer jokes that the only crime here is that the teacher is not having sex with him, while the ranking officer states they should track Kyle's brother down to give him his "luckiest boy in America" medal.

South Park regularly addresses real life issues, and the episode accurately displays the double standard held in popular culture towards sex crimes in education where the defendant is female. To be clear, most perpetrators in reported sex crimes are men. Female offenders account for approximately 10 percent of all sex crimes reported to authorities. When measuring sex crimes involving teachers and students however, women are far more active. Over 30% of all teacher/student misconduct include women as the offenders. While male offenders still outnumber females, the number of female offenders being charged are on the rise because they are finally being reported to police instead of just being whispered about in locker rooms.

But despite being apprehended, there are clear differences in the way male offenders are being treated in the judicial system in contrast to their female counterparts who are deemed attractive. Female teachers quite often receive "sweetheart deals" that are far from equitable to those male teachers receive. And if we start with analyzing the media sources that craft our societal view of sex crimes committed by attractive female educators, we have a good starting point to understand the advantage some of these women have in the courtroom.

In July 2020, another Kentucky teacher would make national headlines. Mollie Verkamp taught high school in Walton-Verona High

School where she admitted to sending sexually charged messages and having sex with one of her 17-year-old students. Like clockwork, commentators would flock to the story, making comments like "why did I never get lucky like that in high school?" and "dad is probably high-fiving, saying that's my boy." One the most telling comments states:

"This is so stupid. She didn't rape anyone. And what if the age of the boy and her were reversed and she was 17. I bet his parents wouldn't be putting him behind bars, but I'm guessing that they are going to stick it to her though. That's BS."

While this comment shows a general misunderstanding of the law, it also shows the minimization of a sex crime. To understand this minimization, we must look at its roots.

The Fetishization of Sex Crimes

It does not take too much effort to find websites that fetishize sex crimes committed by women deemed attractive. Since 2009, Barstool Sports have produced their Sex Scandal Starting Lineup. The lists rank female teachers who have been involved in some sort of sexual misconduct with their students in the calendar year. The lists boast "teachers from around the world, of every color," ranked by their attractiveness and entertaining nature of their story. In response to potential criticism the site may receive from "someone who thinks the idea of a hot older woman throwing her life away to bone a teenager is no laughing matter," column writer Jerry Thornton directs detractors to a scene from the popular coming of age movie, American Pie. Of the scene, Thornton says, "so when Stifler's mom told Finch she likes her scotch aged 18 years and then banged him on a pool table, I take it you ran out of the theater? Riiighttt." (This statement fails to defend the list, however, as the character of Finch was aged at 18 and Stifler's mom was not an authority figure to him. But I digress.)

Meanwhile, the website Boredazzle boasts their own list. Titled "10 Hottest Teachers Caught Sleeping with Their Students," the website equates acts of sexual misconduct between female teachers and students, with the joy of finishing a difficult video game. At Boredazzle, a male student being sexually assaulted by an attractive teacher is like "beating the last level of Tetris when the pieces are moving insanely fast." To the site's credit, they do touch on the criminal charges these women picked up, but they still view these stories of sexual assault as "the perfect storm" of lucky students meeting sexually willing teachers.

Pornography is another outlet that continues the female teacher-male student fantasy. Adult website, RedTube, reports that the term "sexy teacher" is one of their most common searched terms. Surprisingly, their statistics show that women are 17% more likely to search for pornography featuring teachers. Men however, tend to get more specific in their searches with the terms "MILF teacher" and "Japanese teacher" being the two most searched sub-categories. Regarding age ranges, the college aged 18–24 demographic logs in the most searches. But the statistics clearly show that the teacher/student fantasy is popular with all age groups and, apparently, sexes.

Even law and crime-based outlets are guilty of the fetishization of female sexual predators. True Crime Daily is an investigative website that reports true crime news. Their video entitled "Iowa Teacher Fired for Sex with Student Turns to Stripping, Pornography" tells the story of Mary Beth Haglin. Haglin was a substitute teacher engaged in a sexual relationship with one of her 17-year-old students. The narrator of the video makes sure to remind the audience of Haglin's attractiveness. In the 18-minute video, the convicted sex offender is referred to as "pretty" twice, "saucy" three times and "beautiful" once. Haglin's crime, sexual exploitation by a school employee, is downplayed throughout the video, being referred to as "naughty after school activities," a "steamy affair," and a "naughty romance." Also troubling is the way the boy is characterized. The narrator refers to him as a "boy toy" twice, "teenage lover" twice as well as "underage lover," "student lover," "young lover," and "teen dream boy" throughout the video. Only once is he referred to as a "victim of a sex crime." While most videos on the site are presented as serious crime stories, Haglin's is presented as something more at home on the Jerry Springer or Maury show.

The lighthearted and flattering coverage that female offenders receive in the media bathes them in the light of pop culture sensations instead of being categorized as the vile sexual predators their male counterparts are. This fetishization minimizes the victimization of young boys, often times leading to them being less likely to come forward for fear of embarrassment. The fetishization and double standard carries into the judicial system as well. After all, our attorneys, judges, and jury members are all a part of this society that diminishes the harm done to male victims while making pop culture stars of their female abusers.

Judicial Diminishment

Not only are there differences in the way sexual assault cases are viewed in popular media, there is also a difference in the way female defendants are treated judicially, in comparison to their male counterparts. Although the potential criminal penalties are the same regardless of gender, and the alleged actions are similar, in many cases female teacher offenders face lighter criminal penalties than their male counterparts. There is no shortage of cases that highlight the leniency attractive female teachers receive for their crimes.

Take for instance, Kentucky teacher Lindsey Banta Jarvis. Jarvis made headlines in 2018 when she was convicted of third-degree rape and third-degree sodomy of a student younger than 16. In 2016, the Woodford and Fayette County educator had sex with a 15-year-old student. Jarvis received the light sentence of only 18 months incarceration for her crimes. The smirk that Jarvis wore in her mugshot suggests she knew her fate would not be that severe.

One could certainly understand a smirk of confidence from a female defendant as other examples of light sentencing have set the precedent that the attractive fare better in court. For instance, in October 2011 Andrea Conners, a teacher at Highland High School in Fort Thomas, Kentucky, carried on a two-month sexual relationship with a 17-year-old student. Conners faced five years imprisonment but only served 90 days. Similarly in 2015, Madison Southern High School teacher, Brandi Lynn Vaughn had sex with a 16-year-old student — once in the teacher's home and once in a state park. Vaughn faced two counts of first-degree sexual abuse, two counts of third-degree sodomy, one count each of third-degree rape, and evidence tampering. Those charges were dropped with Vaughn pleading guilty to the lesser charge of using an electronic device to induce a minor to engage in sexual activities. As with Andrea Conners, Vaughn faced a five-year sentence, but only received 90 days imprisonment. While media does its part in advancing the idea that these crimes committed by female teachers are not as serious as those committed by males, light sentences like these continue to advance the idea, judicially.

While the sentencing of these crimes make a loud statement, the actual words from judges contribute to their diminishment as well. In 2014, Pennsylvania teacher Erica Ann Ginnetti sent photos and videos of herself — clad in a bikinis and thongs — to a 17-year-old student. She later had sex with the student. Ginnetti pled guilty to sexual assault and disseminating sexual materials, charges that carry a maximum of seven to fourteen years' incarceration. Ginnetti received a sentence of 30 days of jail time. At her sentencing, Judge Garett Page referred to the sexual material she sent to the student as "dangling candy."

These reduced sentences don't just diminish the importance of the crime for the offenders but also send a troubling message to the victims. Through low sentences and the judges' minimization of these crimes, judges also invalidate the depression, low self-esteem, and relationship difficulties that boys may face as consequences of sexual abuse. Again, many examples of this effect exist. In 2005, Sandra "Beth" Geisel, a high school teacher from Christian Brothers Academy in Albany, New York, was charged with the statutory rape of a 16-year-old student. In 2004, Geisel raped the student in her home as well as in the press box of the school's football field. After initially claiming she was forced into sexual acts by the student, she eventually admitted to the crime, receiving a sentence of only 6 months in jail and 10 years' probation. After handing down that light sentence, Judge Stephen Herrick sympathized with Geisel, claiming she was a victim, too. The judge then proceeded to downplay the effect the rape had on the student, stating:

"The 16- year-old is a victim in the statutory sense only. He certainly was not victimized by you in any sense of the word... You misunderstood attention as affection and failed to realize you were being manipulated and sexually abused, and you became a playmate.

Obviously, the 16-year-old's parents were furious with this response from a judicial official elected to serve justice. But Judge Herrick's statement is no different than the typical utterances of "luckiest boy in the world," and "I wish that were me" found in social media comment sections, their similarities a byproduct of the same fetishizing society.

Judges are not the only ones displaying fetishization in court, as attorneys have exploited double standards for their female client's advantage during hearings. In 2004, Tampa teacher Debra LaFave was accused of and arrested for having sex numerous times with one of her students. The student in question was 14 years old. LaFave was charged with four felony counts of lewd and lascivious battery and one count of lewd and lascivious exhibition. LaFave's attorney, John Fitzgibbons, called the court to take his client's "platinum blond hair and ice blue eyes" into consideration stating:

"To place Debbie into a Florida state women's penitentiary, to place an attractive young woman in that kind of hellhole, is like putting a piece of raw meat in with the lions."

Fitzgibbon's argument was successful; LaFave ultimately received three years of house arrest and seven years of probation. Once again, society's admiration for the attractive female diminished the seriousness of the crime, proven by LaFave's obscenely light punishment.

It is true that there are exceptions to the double standard. Joseph Ruggieri from Pennsylvania's Plum High School only received 2–5 years for having sex with a 16-year-old student in his car in 2016. In contrast, Brittany Zamora, a teacher from Las Brisas Academy in Arizona, was sentenced to 20 years in prison for having sex multiple times with a 13-year-old boy in 2019. However despite the instances where the double standard is reversed, the above cases highlight the advantage female offenders may have when facing justice. When one looks at how normalized the fantasy of the "lusty teacher hook-up" has become, it is easy to understand how legal officers may be tempted to show leniency to female offenders. Officers of the law are not exempt from a culture that fetishizes attractive female offenders. Rather, they too are members of that culture which views female sexual offenses as "rites of passage" into manhood for the male victim, instead of the crimes they truly are.

Conclusion

If you Google Ramsey Bearse, one of the first pictures that pop up is a composite image. On the left side is a tearful mugshot, and on the right is Bearse, clad in a pink bikini at one of her beauty pageants. In my research for this essay, I was unable to locate any similar photos of male offenders; a teary mug shot juxtaposed with a picture of the predator running shirtless on the beach, a la David Hasselhoff from Baywatch. And try as I might, I was unable to find any "Top 10 Hottest Male Sex Offenders" lists; with male child molesters who have been entrusted with the wellbeing of children, staring back lustfully at the camera. Given the societal double standard, it is not hard to understand why. In our society, male sexual offenders are monsters and female sex offenders are intriguing. And in a media driven world where sex sells, headlines that tout "sex romps with hot teachers" are the ones that garner clicks and attract traffic to the websites that bear them. Though the headlines are salacious and attention-grabbing, they play a significant role in devaluing not only the trauma that male survivors endure, but also the justice they deserve. In no criminal law textbook are pouty lips and bewitching eyes defenses for sexual assault, nor should they be. There is a reason why Lady Justice wears a blindfold.

4

---·---

YEEZY TAUGHT ME: KANYE WEST AND THE CHARACTERISTICS OF ABUSE

With perhaps the exception of 50 Cent, there was no bigger name in 2000s hip hop than Kanye West. West's seminal 2004 album, "The College Dropout", single handily led a massive shift in the genre. Kanye used his brashness to carve a space in mainstream rap for topics such as self-consciousness, religion, and the failings of the American higher education system, at a time where the hypermasculine themes found in the music of his contemporaries like Cam'Ron, Ludacris, and the aforementioned 50 Cent, ruled the Top 40 airwaves.

The early 2000s also saw the rise of another culture shifter; one Kim Kardashian. Daughter of OJ Simpson dream team attorney Robert Kardashian, Kim first gained fame as the friend and stylist of socialite, Paris Hilton, appearing a handful of times on her reality show, "The Simple Life" from 2003 to 2006. The nonconsensual leaking of a sex tape with R&B singer Ray J, would make Kardashian a household name in 2007.

Kanye and Kim would marry in 2014. With Kanye being one of the most famed and decorated artists in hip hop history and Kim becoming a reality TV icon and successful businesswoman, the two were seemingly a perfect match in celebrity heaven, eventually parenting four children.

In 2021, Kardashian filed for divorce from West. While the dissolution of a marriage isn't uncommon, the typical divorce doesn't play out in public forums such as *TMZ* and *US Weekly*. As Kanye and Kim's entire relationship occurred in front of paparazzi and reality TV cameras however, it comes as no surprise that the public would have a front row ticket to the relationship's end as well.

While many followed the star couple's separation for entertainment purposes, the public nature of the divorce displayed alarming behavior for advocates in the domestic violence world. Women Safe, INC highlights 12 common characteristics of an abuser. The list of traits includes controlling, charming, jealous, inconsistent, manipulative, threatening, demanding, blames the victim, attacks self-esteem, isolation, rigid gender roles, and destruction of property. And some of these traits were clearly present as Kim herself described Kanye's behavior through their divorce as controlling and manipulative.

To be clear, it has never been alleged that Kanye West has ever physically assaulted his wife or any other woman for that matter. Physical violence, however, isn't always a requisite for domestic violence. The United States Department of Justice defines domestic violence as "a pattern of abusive behaviors in any relationship that are used by one partner to gain or maintain power and control over another intimate partner. It involves a pattern of coercive behavior in intimate relationships whereby the behavior is controlled through humiliation, intimidation, fear, and often intentional physical, emotional or sexual injury." And when we look at some of West's public behavior during (and even before) his divorce from Kim, many of his actions align with some of the typical warning signs of nonphysical domestic abuse.

Coercive Control

For those who followed Kim and Kanye's relationship, his coercive controlling behavior during the couple's divorce shouldn't come as a surprise. One of the earliest instances of this control can be seen in West's dominion over his wife's appearance. Prior to meeting West, Kim dressed in the same multicolored bandaged dresses, glittery accessories, and leopard-printed pumps as her Los Angeles reality television contemporaries. Once the two began dating however, Kanye notoriously engineered rebrand of Kim's closet, informing her that she had "the worst style". In a memorable 2012 scene from her reality show, "Keeping Up with the Kardashian's", Kim begged to keep certain items of clothing as Kanye threw out the pieces of her wardrobe he didn't approve of and replaced them with clothes that reflected *his* high fashion aesthetic. With the whimsical background music, the scene was played in a lighthearted nature. And some critics point to this moment being a crucial part of Kim's overall evolution. Fashion website *InStyle* would ponder how Kim would dress without Kanye in control once their marriage had ended. But Kanye's closet takeover, shows as a common characteristic of abuse.

Emma Davey, who is a narcissistic abuse expert and founder of the UK based counseling firm My Trauma Therapy, defines coercive control as a form of psychological abuse whereby the perpetrator carries out a pattern of controlling and manipulative behaviors within a relationship and exerts power over a victim, often through intimidation or humiliation, which tends to be more subtle and harder to spot. Policing one's lifestyle through the "rebrand" of their wardrobe falls into these behaviors. "It may seem caring if your partner shows interest in your fashion choices or likes to know where you are at all times. But if they tell you how to dress or where to go, this is a common sign of coercive control", says Davey.

Kanye's control over Kim's appearance was more than just a one-off spot for a reality show. Kim has previously stated that Kanye not only told her what to wear, but also made her change her outfit if he didn't like it. In a 2016 *GQ* article, Kanye told Kim that the one thing that drives him crazy in their relationship is when Kim forgets to email Kanye sketches of the ensembles that designers send her. A 2013 article in *US Magazine* perhaps highlights the extent of the influence Kanye had in this area as Kim stated, "I dress for Kanye West more than for myself." And it appears this behavior was not just limited to Kardashian. After mere days of meeting Julia Fox on New Year's Eve 2021, Kanye had replaced all of actress' clothes with a new wardrobe, once again, matching *his* tastes. "After meeting him, a couple days later, all of my shit was in boxes, gone", says Fox. This rightfully caused some to question if Kanye was controlling Fox in the same way he did Kim.

Kanye's other major control play was his post-divorce choice of residence. In late December 2021, it was reported that Kanye purchased a home directly across the street from Kim. Kanye claimed that the purpose of the move was to be a constant presence in his children's' life. Per statements from Kardashian, it did not appear that the two parents were in agreement of the arrangement as Kim stated was "not thrilled" about the proximity of her ex.

To unpack why this move is less the actions of a loving father and more a behavior of abuse, it's important to look once again at coercive control. In addition to policing your partner's appearance, another behavior of coercive control is monitoring your partner's activity through the day, which is easy to do when just a glance out your kitchen window will let you know who is coming and going from your exe's house at any given time. Kanye's actions here definitely did not fool domestic abuse experts. "How many amazing dads do you know who stay present in their child's life without moving to their ex's street?", says El Hoffman, a Louisville based domestic abuse consultant. "It has nothing to do with his kids and everything to do with the need to keep an intensive eye on Kim so that he can continue to exert his manipulative control", she continues. Hoffman reflects the belief of many that the life Kanye wanted to be a "constant presence" in was in fact Kim's.

Jealousy

Another common trait found in domestic abusers is jealousy. "When it comes to abusers, jealousy manifests from their need to control", says Hoffman. "Deep inside they are wounded juveniles trapped in full grown adult bodies and anything that threatens their power becomes their target to take down", she continues. And for Kanye, Kim's new boyfriend was right in his crosshairs.

The first photos of Kim holding hands with comedian Pete Davidson, surfaced on October 31st, 2021. From then, thanks to the ever-present paparazzi, pictures were published of Kim and Pete canoodling in New York, dining in Beverly Hills, and boarding private planes to the Bahamas. The relationship also caused Kanye to exhibit the abusive characteristic of jealousy in response.

Hoffman states that abusers will make fun of or try to discredit anything that can be seen as competition. As Kanye is still at his core, a rapper, it's no surprise that he would attack Pete in song. He made subliminal insults to Pete like the one in the Fivio Foreign and Alicia Keys assisted song "City of Gods" where Kanye rapped:

"This afternoon, a hundred goons pullin' up to SNL/When I pull up, it's dead-on arrival."

Some of the threats were more straight forward like in the song "Eazy" where Kanye rapped:

"God saved me from that crash/just so I can beat Pete Davidson's ass."

Should these lyrics be taken as actual threats? Kanye certainly wouldn't be the first person to rap about things he never planned to do. And the thought of needing "a hundred goons" to inflict bodily harm on the equivalent of the nicest stoner on campus, is a laughable thought. But Kanye's jealous behavior extended past a few verses in a couple of throw away songs.

In January 2022, reports revealed that Kanye was spreading a false rumor that Davidson had the AIDS virus. Kanye began ex-communicating other colleagues such as long-standing collaborator and fellow musician Kid Cudi, due to their friendship with Davidson. And then there was Kanye's social media campaign against Davidson in which he took to Instagram and Twitter to lob playground insults like calling Pete a "dickhead" and bestowing Davidson with the nickname "Skete Davidson" ("skeet" being a slang term for semen).

Hoffman states, "the terrifying thing is too often these tactics can empower something much more deadly." This is something that Kardashian understood as she sent Kanye a text, warning him that his antics were "creating a dangerous and scary environment in which someone would hurt Pete and it will be all his fault." Of course, Kanye promptly publicly shared this text along with an Instagram picture of actor Ving Rhames putting fellow actor Tyrese Gibson in a choke hold (a scene from the 2001 movie Baby Boy) barring a caption that read:

"UPON MY WIFE'S REQUEST, PLEASE NOBODY DO ANYTHING PHYSICAL TO SKETE. I'M GOING TO HANDLE THIS SITUATION MYSELF."

Blaming the Victim

Blaming one's victims is yet another characteristic common in abusers. Counselors have stated that this is psychological trick abusers pull where they try to shift the blame for the abusive situation onto their victims and simultaneously paint themselves as the true victims who are suffering cruel, unfair attacks at the hands of the very people they are abusing. Not only is this another behavior Kanye has indulged in, he used his and Kim's children as the battle ground.

In November 2021, Kim and her eldest daughter North, launched a joint Tik Tok account for them both to have a little mother-daughter fun on social media with. Kanye however, didn't' take kindly to this as he made an Instagram post on February 4th, 2022, stating:

"SINCE THIS IS MY FIRST DIVORCE, I NEED TO KNOW WHAT I SHOULD DO ABOUT MY DAUGHTER BEING PUT ON TIK TOK AGAINST MY WILL?

Now, as North's father, Kanye certainly is entitled to a say in his daughter's life. However, two elements of post, showed that perhaps this was more of a gaslighting expedition than the "innocent message" Kanye wanted us to believe it was.

First, look at the language Kanye used. Using phrases such as *"my* first divorce" and "against *my* will" show that this post is more about West being the victim than it is about his child. Secondly, why did this have to be a public post in the first place? Certainly, this is something that could have been discussed in private between the two parents. Did Kanye's 10 million Instagram followers *really* need to know about this?

Elsewhere, Kanye also accused Kim of "kidnapping" another one of their daughters. On February 4th, 2022, West once again took to his Instagram page to publicly air out his frustrations with not being included in his daughter Chicago's 4th birthday party. Kanye accused

Kim of "kidnapping" their daughter by refusing to share with him the address of the party. Kanye would then claim that once he found out where the party was being held, Kim "put security on him inside of the house to play with his son and then accused him of stealing." In Kim's response to these accusations, she revealed that the idea to have separate parties was Kanye's to begin with.

Kanye waging these co-parenting wars in public was done for one specific reason; to paint the narrative that Kanye is the victim and Kim is the villain. And this is a play right out of the abuser playbook. A 2017 article in *Evolution Counseling* describes this strategy saying, "abusers will make overgeneralizations, take things out of context, find a grain of truth, or just flat out lie in order to spin a deceptive tale of the things their victims have said and done or haven't said and done, a deceptive tale that supposedly proves the hostile, ungrateful, lazy, arrogant, cruel, abusive, etc. natures of their victims." The article goes on to say, "at this point most victims, their heads spinning, feel compelled to defend their own past comments, their own past behaviors, their own way of being in the world! In other words, the situation reverts right back to business as usual, to the abusive situation."

Wake Up, Mr. West

As with most celebrities, wearing the rose-colored glasses of fanship made it hard for some to truly grasp the gravity of Kanye's actions. But Kanye provided us with a real time case study on the type of non-violent domestic abuse that contributes to the more than 10 million domestic assaults per year.

As for Kanye himself, one would hope that the man that helped so many gawky undergrads find their self-confidence through his music in the early 2000s, would be able to wake up and see the toxicity of the model of masculinity that he not only exhibited for the world but, also for his very own son.

Whether he did or not, remains to be seen.

5

ATTORNEYS SAY THE DARNDEST THINGS

A ttorneys are often considered pillars of their communities. Often thought of as vigorous champions of justice, attorneys are bound by their rules of professional responsibility to be zealous advocates on their client's behalf. Sometimes though, zealous advocacy leads to the absurd. And when it does, three years of professional school is not enough to keep bizarre statements from escaping a counselor's lips. Often desperate, commonly offensive, and always cringe-worthy, here are some of the darndest things attorneys have said about sexual assault.

It's No Longer the Sixties

We start in 2015, in the middle of Donald Trump's Presidential campaign. While the eventual President has no shortage of his own questionable comments, this nugget of legal incorrectness comes from his then-lawyer, Michael Cohen. While defending the future 45th President from a decades old allegation that he forced himself on his then wife Ivana Trump, Cohen would state:

"You're talking about the front-runner for the GOP, presidential candidate, as well as a private individual who never raped anybody.

And, of course, understand that by the very definition, you can't rape your spouse. You cannot rape your spouse. And there's very clear case law."

There was actually a time when this statement would have been correct. The 1962 Model Penal Code qualified rape in the United States as an act perpetrated by a male against a female who was not his wife. In the early 1970's, laws would be changed to require a husband and wife to no longer be living together in order for rape charges to be brought, with *Oregon v. Rideout* being the first case to challenge this cohabitation clause. While the husband in that case would ultimately be acquitted, the case placed a spotlight on marital rape and, by 1993, all 50 states had made marital rape illegal (despite there being some loopholes in some states' laws).

Cohen's statement is interesting because he graduated from Michigan's Thomas M. Cooley Law School in 1991, three years after the state made marital rape illegal. Therefore, you could absolutely rape your spouse the entire time Cohen was in law school. Surely, his criminal law professor must have mentioned this as it would have been a brand-new state law his 1L year.

Cohen must not have paid much attention in his Professional Responsibilities class either as he was disbarred in 2019 for making false statements to Congress.

Non-Expert Opinion

Our next story takes us to 2020. As Cuba Gooding Jr's acting career started in the late 1980's, there is a variety of projects that may make his name a familiar one, including his Academy Award winning turn as Rod Tidwell in 1996's Jerry Maguire or his breakthrough performance as Tre Styles in 1991's Boyz n the Hood. My personal favorite performance from Gooding was his role as former football star, "alleged" murderer, and convicted Las Vegas heist puller, OJ.

Simpson in 2016's American Crime Story: The People vs OJ Simpson. This essay, however, isn't a movie review; it's an analysis on bizarre things attorneys say. And as such we look at Gooding's attorney, Peter Toumbekis.

In June 2019, Gooding was arrested when a woman accused the actor of groping her breasts at a posh Times Square bar. This initial accusation led to a total of 30 separate women lobbing groping accusations at the actor and one woman coming forward with a rape accusation from 2013. On August 13th, 2020, Gooding's legal team met with prosecutors at a preliminary hearing, where Toumbekis flexed his muscle as an unlicensed psychologist. When asked by Judge Curtis Farber if Toumbekis planned to ask a line of questioning about a witnesses bra size, Toumbekis replied that he in fact, did plan on asking these questions, arguing that small breasted women can be delusional and their low self-esteem can incorrectly lead them to believe they have been assaulted.

As unfounded as this argument sounds on its face, my degree is in law, not psychology. So, I did what Toumbekis failed to do: I asked an expert. "To be blunt: no research whatsoever supports this notion," says Dr. Dede Wohlfarth. Dr. Wohlfarth is the Director of the Child, Adolescent and Family Emphasis Area of Spalding University's Psychology program. Her treatment philosophy is evidence-based and practical, two things that Toumbekis' argument is not. "I know of absolutely no research that suggests that low self-esteem can make a person be delusional and falsely claim sexual abuse," Dr. Wohlfarth continues. "Usually in psychology, we say 'maybe/it depends on the context' but this one... it is a no. Nada. No research support for this."

Just as Dr. Wohlfarth rejects this theory, so did Judge Farber, who barred Toumbekis from this line of questioning. With both the psychological and legal worlds rejecting Cuba's strategy, his case got off to a *fantastic* start.

That's not how childbirth works, Leon!

Our last story takes us to the glorious decade of neon colors and pop music that was the 80s. Anytime a story begins with a person on a crusade against women's rights, you can go ahead and expect something offensive from the start. But that is the exact crusade that then-law clerk James Leon Holmes was on at the turn of the decade. In 1980, Holmes wrote a letter in favor of a constitutional ban on abortion. One longstanding argument in favor of legal abortions is that it protects survivors who become pregnant with their rapist's child. Holmes disagreed with this stance however, stating "concern for rape victims is a red herring because conceptions from rape occur with approximately the same frequency as snowfall in Miami."

As outlandish as this statement sounds, Holmes would not be alone in stating that rape victims cannot get pregnant from sexual assault. In 1988, State Representative Stephen Freind expanded on Holmes' theory, stating that rape victims rarely become pregnant "because they secrete a chemical that kills sperm." Seven years later in 1995, Republican Representative Henry Aldridge, in an effort to eliminate state abortion funds for poor women, publicly stated that women do not get pregnant when raped because "the juices don't flow" during an attack. Two decades later, Missouri Republican Todd Akin would sink his political career by saying that "victims of legitimate rape very rarely get pregnant because their bodies prevent them from doing so." While Holmes' remark would do very little to derail his legal career (which would take him to the level of Senior Judge of the United States District Court for the Eastern District of Arkansas), by 2012 the public showed it was not having any this same foolishness from Akin, as he lost his bid to unseat Senator Claire McCaskill due to the remark.

Not only does "rape victims can't get pregnant" fly in the face of common sense, it also flies in the face of everything I learned in my junior high school sex ed class. Were all of these "intelligent" men privy to an alternative curriculum? It turns out that this theory goes all the way back to the 13th century. 1290's Fleta, one of the earliest British legal texts stated "if, however, the woman should have conceived at the time alleged in the appeal, it abates, for without a woman's consent she could not conceive." While Holmes is usually credited for bringing this archaic theory into abortion politics, in 2003 (16 years after the fact) he would publicly apologize for his "strident and harsh" rhetoric.

Better late than never, I suppose.

Bonus Track: "I Absolutely Don't Understand What You Are Talking About"

Despite one of my editor's opinions otherwise, no list of "what the heck were they thinking" court statements would be complete without including the Brock Turner "Outercourse" defense.

By the time attorney Eric Multhaup appeared before a California appellate court in 2018, his client Brock Turner, had already succeeded in becoming the poster boy for collegiate sexual assault and white privilege. After being convicted of sexually assaulting Chanel Miller, Turner would be sentenced to only six months in jail; a move that would ultimately lead to trial Judge Aaron Persky being recalled and also fired as a high school tennis coach.

Despite only serving half of his already ridiculously low sentence, Turner would seek an appeal in an effort to avoid registering as a sex offender for life. It was at the appeal hearing that Multhaup argued that not only was there not enough evidence to convict Turner, but all his client was guilty of was "sexual outercourse" as his pants remained on during the assault.

While I am certainly familiar with sexual INTERcourse, sexual outercourse was a new term to me, so I did my Googles for further research. Healthline describes sexual outercourse as an ambiguous activity, meaning different things to different people. Included in the list of activities that count as outercourse are kissing, massage, mutual masturbation, oral sex, anal sex, and Turner's pastime of choice, dry humping. Multhap attempted to convince the Court that as Brock was only dry humping Chanel Miller, he was not exposed and therefore not in a position to complete the act of rape.

I can see what Multhap was trying to do here. It is true that dry humping can be considered its own, low risk alternative to intercourse; a point Multhap was trying to prove as a defense to Turner's "Assault with Intent to Rape" Conviction. While it is true that dry humping can exist on its own, it is also true that all forms of outercourse can serve as foreplay before sexual intercourse. The Appellate Court agreed, pointing out that while Turner was clothed and only dry humping at the time he was interrupted by the graduate students that found him, a reasonable juror using commonsense, could easily infer that if the grad students had not stopped Turner, who grinding away atop of an unconscious women whose underwear had been removed, and who he had previously digitally penetrated, exposure and rape were right around the corner. The original judgment was upheld.

A Little Research Goes a Long Way

It's interesting how powerful the smallest bit of research can be. It can save you from claiming a long-outdated rule as current. It can also spare you from showing your complete lack of knowledge of the female anatomy. And if these stories tell us anything, it's that for attorneys, legal research is a practice that should extend long past the years of law school. It is also a practice that should not be 100% delegated to overworked law clerks. And who knows, it just may save you from being the butt of public ridicule when someone is writing an article about attorneys that have gotten sexual assault all wrong.

6

PLEASE DON'T SHARE THESE: A REVENGE PORN PRIMER

Melissa

"Hey, there are some naked pictures of you online."

That is not a text message most people would like to get, but it was a reality for Melissa. "About three or four years ago, I met a guy online," Melissa said. "We flirted for a couple of months and somewhere in there, I sent him some nude photos at his request." To Melissa, sending a few nude pictures wasn't that big of a deal. She even forgot she had sent them for a while.

Then the text messages started.

"All of the sudden, my phone was blowing up with messages left and right about me being online naked," Melissa said. She quickly went to the sites her friends told her about and sure enough, there they were. "I was shocked! I had sent something to someone I trusted in private. Now here it was for the whole world to see."

Melissa confronted the guy she had talked to online, asking why he shared her images. Although he claimed he didn't do it, there was no one else she shared those particular pictures with. "At first I cried.

Cried out of anger at myself for sending the pictures in the first place," she recalled. Today, she takes a different approach to the situation.

"Okay. They're out there. It sucks. It is what it is."

But Melissa also lives in the continual shadow that looms over her head due to the photos.

"You never know when you're having a conversation, a date, or a job interview with someone who has seen you naked."

A Better Name

From its beginnings in the form of stolen nude photos in the pages of a 1980 issue of Hustler Magazine, to dedicated websites of the modern day, revenge porn has been used to make the private moments of many public. Revenge porn is defined as "the sharing of private, sexual materials, either photos or videos, of another person without their consent and with the purpose of causing embarrassment or distress." Psychologists have pointed to the desire to "get back" at someone who has hurt you as the reason that people share revenge porn; it is the ultimate ability to hurt and embarrass someone.

While "revenge porn" is the most frequently used term, it creates a narrow view as to why these images and videos are shared. While some perpetrators do seek to embarrass ex romantic partners, many are not motivated by vengeance or personal feelings towards the victim. When asked why she thought the man she met online shared her nude photos, Melissa stated that his actions "weren't out of spite but rather, out of opportunity." Images have been used for a variety of different reasons other than revenge such as trade for the nude photos of others and ransom from the victim in the picture. As such, the term "nonconsensual pornography" is a better description of the crime.

Nonconsensual pornography is defined as the distribution of sexually graphic images of individuals without their consent and is a term that is broad enough to capture the multiple motivations behind sharing one's naked photos.

Lisa, Nathaly, and Nicole

While Melissa's story is not enviable, it is one that many have experienced. A study from the Data and Society Research Institute has shown that around 10 million Americans have either been threatened with or have been victims of nonconsensual image sharing.

Lisa from Massachusetts shares the same anxiety that Melissa does when it comes to never knowing exactly who has seen her naked. Lisa was 17 when her then boyfriend took topless photos of her without her knowledge. Lisa states that she didn't even know her boyfriend owned a camera. Years later, her photos were posted online. The pictures spread quickly in Lisa's small town, reaching people she saw on a daily basis. "There is nothing you can do about it," Lisa states. "It's just there, and you can't take it down, and you don't know who has seen it." Melissa agrees, stating "you lose the power over who gets to see you naked. That choice is stolen from you." Living in a small town also amplifies the anxiety victims feel. "When you live in a small town, there is far less anonymity," Melissa states. "The kid bagging your groceries could have very well have seen you nude and you'll never know."

While hometown anxiety is certainly a heavy burden to carry, in some cases there are professional opportunities in danger of being ruined by the posting of non-consensual pornography. While preparing to compete in the 2017 Miss New York USA Pageant, Nathaly Rodriguez began receiving phone calls and text messages from an ex-boyfriend threatening to post nude pictures and videos of her online. Nathaly initially thought that he was bluffing. She quickly realized this was no joke however, when she received a link to the porn website where he posted a video of the two having sex as well as details that would easily allow viewers to discover it was her. "He knew about me running in the pageant and he wanted to make sure I would never have a chance at winning," Rodriguez said. In the fallout of the posting, Rodriguez reported being unable to sleep, eat, or work, as well as having thoughts of suicide.

Non-consensual sexual images have also been used for revenge by scorned third parties as well. During my tenure serving as a university hearing committee member, we had a case come before us where William, a male member of the school's cross country team was accused (and ultimately found responsible) for videotaping himself having sex with Nicole, one of his female teammates without her knowledge or consent.[1] The video came to Nicole's attention when William's girlfriend Tasha found the video and posted it on Twitter to get back at William. While I'm certain that Tasha acted out of the hurt of infidelity, her act of posting the video violated both William and Nicole. When asked, Tasha stated she had no idea that her actions were in fact against university policy.

Martin

Like all sex crimes, the victims are not just limited to females. Martin and Maureen were college sweethearts that eventually married and lived a life which included a large house and a successful business. Maureen's control over Martin started out lightly with phone calls to keep tabs on him and "jokey" threats that she would "ruin his life" if he didn't obey her wishes. The abuse in their marriage would grow however, to include her hacking his phone to isolate him from his family and friends. After their divorce was final, Maureen posted nude images of Martin on Facebook and also emailed them to his family and friends. Martin states that the damage this caused was "irreversible," ruining his reputation, diminishing his income, and harming his business. Even after this, Maureen continued to use the images as a blackmail chip to acquire the legal rights to their home and shared business.

Studiesshow that while women under 30, minorities, and members of the LGBTQ community are more likely to be threatened with revenge porn than men, about 25% of nonconsensual porn victims are men. Of that percentage, nine out of 10 of them are also victims of "sextortion." Sextortion is defined as a form of nonconsenual porn that involves financially blackmailing the victim on top of the humiliation of being exposed online. And while Martin did report his situation to authorities, 81% of men do not report their cases. The reasons men don't report nonconsensual porn cases aren't much different than the reasons they don't report other sexual crimes as embarrassment and fear of ridicule from other men stand as barriers.

Celebrities and Marines

Nonconsensual pornography is not just limited to small incidents. There have been several examples that show just how widespread the practice of sharing sexual images of others is. On August 31, 2014, a large collection of private images and videos of various female celebrities were posted on the 4chan imageboard site. Christened The Fappening (a combination of the word "fap", a slang term for masturbation, and the word "happening"), celebrities including Jennifer Lawrence, Kate Upton, Kirsten Dunst, Rhianna, and Hope Solo found their nude images leaked to the site. After their initial posting, the photos would be reposted to other internet message boards (such as Reddit) and a variety of websites created specifically for sharing the pictures; many of which are still active today.

While some celebrities such as singer Arianna Grande and actresses Victoria Justice and Yvonne Strahovski would claim that the pictures posted of them were fake, others would admit the authenticity of their photos. Actress Mary Elizabeth Winstead stated that her pictures were taken by her husband years ago in the privacy of their home. As the pictures had been previously deleted, Winstead stated that a large amount of effort must have went into finding them. Model Kate Upton called the posting of her pictures an "outrageous violation of her privacy" and threatened legal action for those behind the leak. And while nude photos of celebrities being leaked to the public isn't necessarily a new phenomenon, actress Jennifer Lawrence would highlight the seriousness of this specific leak, saying:

"It is not a scandal. It is a sex crime. It is a sexual violation. It's disgusting. The law needs to be changed, and we need to change. That's why these Web sites are responsible. Just the fact that somebody can be sexually exploited and violated, and the first thought that crosses somebody's mind is to make a profit from it. It's so beyond me. I just can't imagine being that detached from humanity. I can't imagine being that thoughtless and careless and so empty inside."

While it still isn't known who was responsible for initially posting the images online, the methods that five men used to obtain the images were discovered in an FBI investigation. The US Attorney's Office states that Pennsylvania man, Ryan Collins sent the celebrities emails that appeared to be from Apple and Google, asking them to provide their usernames and passwords. Collins gained access to the accounts and thus, the private photos. Another hacker (working independently of Collins) Edward Majerczyk from Chicago, would use the same phishing scheme to hack into the accounts of 30 celebrities (and many other non-celebrities) gaining access to their private information as well. Through IP address tracking, Emilio Herrera, also from Chicago, was found to have accessed 572 individual iCloud accounts using the phishing scheme. George Garofano, from Connecticut, was also named in the investigation. Unlike the other hackers, Garofano claimed he was forced into the hacking by other, more sophisticated criminals.

Christopher Brannon, a former special education teacher from Virginia, was the latest to be named in the hacking. In addition to using the phishing scheme, Brannon would also survey the social media accounts of his victims to help him answer security questions and gain access to their accounts. In addition to celebrity accounts, Brannon also targeted his then-underaged sister-in-law as well as other students and teachers at his former school. While the FBI would state that while the hackers were unconnected, they were part of the same online network that non-consensually traded these images and videos.

Collins would receive 18 months in Federal prison after pleading guilty to felony hacking. Majerick would plea to the same charge, receiving 9 months imprisonment. Herran would receive 16 months imprisonment while Garofano would receive eight months. Lastly, Brannon would receive 34 months in prison for his role in the breach.

Another large-scale incident involved a branch of the United States Military. In 2017, the United States Department of Defense investigated hundreds of Marines for their part in a secret Facebook group used to share nonconsensual pornography. The group "Marines United" had over 30,000 followers and featured thousands of explicit images of unknowing servicewomen. The images came complete with dossiers of the women which included their names, military branches and rank. Former Marine Corps corporal (and current tattoo model) Elle Audra told The Marine Corps Times of the aftermath she has faced since her pictures were shared. "The messages are usually something around like: 'when were you in?' and 'I would have fucked you too,'" Audra said of the messages she has received from strangers on Facebook. She even received a request for sex from a man who knew the specifics of when and where she was deployed.

Civilians weren't safe from Marines United either. Michigan bartender Kelsi Stone broke up with her Marine boyfriend in 2016. Shortly after, Stone received a text message from a friend alerting her that nude pictures of her had been shared on Facebook. Stone recognized the pictures immediately as she had previously sent them to her then boyfriend while he was away training in California. She would report not only receiving lewd comments on social media, but also receiving in-person harassment from Marines who frequented her bar. Kelsi and Elle's situations aren't unique, as cyberstalking and harassment are both common outcomes of the circulation of nonconsensual nude images. Ultimately, over 100 Marines were punished for their involvement with Marines United.

One of the largest distributors of nonconsensual pornography was the online image board called Anon-IB. The board was founded in 2006 and hosted thousands of images of women, cataloged by the state and country where they live. Anon-IB became notorious, being named "ground zero" in the sharing of the photos from the 2014 Celebrity Leak as well as also being a sharing point for the Marine United photos as well. In 2018, a Dutch Cybercrime team seized the Anon- IB forum as a part of an ongoing investigation. But in 2020 there were reports of someone trying to revive the board, starting a new site that took the name and appearance of the original board. While Anon- IB may be one of the biggest, it is hardly the first website with the sole purpose of sharing revenge porn.

In 2013, suburban mother Ariella Alexander was reported to be the brains behind the shesahomewrecker.com; a website where scorned wives could send nude pictures of their husbands' mistresses for posting and public ridicule. Websites such as thedirty.com and myex.com would follow suit, creating an avenue for and promoting revenge through the sharing of nude photos. In 2012, the FBI would investigate the site, IsAnyoneUp.com. In an interview, the site's creator Hunter Moore would dub himself a "professional life ruin-er" and stated that he wanted to take full advantage of people's mistakes. For the most part, sites will remove pictures at the victim's request. "My pictures will occasionally pop up on a site called Mewes" Melissa says. "I can usually get them removed if I know about them though", she continues. For Melissa and her husband, doing Google searches for her images has become a regular practice. For others though, the process of getting their pictures removed from sites has not been as easy as Melissa's, with some reporting having to pay as much as $500 for removal. While many of these revenge sites still exist, the enactment of state laws have wiped them of the nonconsensual images they once proudly posted.

Legal Stance

The first nonconsensual pornography state laws were introduced in 2013. While Texas, Alaska, and New Jersey already had broad privacy laws that included revenge porn, by the end of 2014, 13 states had passed laws that specifically banned nonconsensual pornography. As of 2020, 46 states as well as Washington DC have enacted laws.[2] However, these laws do not come without challenge.

Minnesota's nonconsensual pornography statute was put into effect on August 1, 2016. Their Nonconsensual Dissemination of Private Sexual Images statute was meant to punish those who intentionally share sexual images intended to be private, without consent. Since its enactment, over 300 people have been charged and over 100 have been convicted under the statute.

In 2018, Michael Anthony Casillas was convicted of felony non-consensual dissemination of private images after he used his victim's password to access her online accounts and retrieve sexual photos and videos of her after their relationship ended. The images would be sent to 44 people and posted online as well. Initially, Casillas received a 23-month sentence. On appeal however, rather than defending Casillas' actions, his attorney John Arechigo would attack the law itself.

Arechigo would argue that the law had been too broadly written, stating that the statue applied a "negligence mens rea" standard, which meant that prosecutors did not have to show that a defendant intended to cause harm. While making sure to highlight that he was not advocating for the right to distribute revenge pornography, Arechigo would argue that the law was unconstitutional as it "sweeps up people who don't have any criminal intent, including people who accidentally disseminate images." And to his credit, this argument worked. While the Court of Appeals would call Casillas' conduct "abhorrent," they would vacate the conviction on the grounds that the statute is unconstitutional, effectively striking down the law. Arechigo would later state:

"The Court of Appeals thoroughly and thoughtfully analyzed the issues and arguments we raised. This case wasn't about whether people should be able to disseminate "revenge porn." It was about the law that Minnesota legislators passed three years ago. The law was poorly written. The law didn't punish an invasion of privacy, as the state argued. The law didn't even require an invasion of privacy as a basis to bring criminal charges. The Court of Appeals properly ruled the law punished speech in violation of the First Amendment. It's up to state legislators to craft better legislation if they're really trying to protect victims of 'revenge porn.'"

The Casillas' case is important because it sets a precedent for other states. As nonconsensual pornography statutes are relatively new laws, it is no surprise that other states would look at Minnesota for guidance in their own legal challenges. In 2020, Indiana's revenge porn law would also be ruled unconstitutional. In March of that year, Trine University student Conner Katz recorded a video of himself in an intimate act with another student in a campus fraternity house. He would later show the video to others. Katz was charged with distribution of an intimate image, a Class A misdemeanor, however the case would be dismissed in October by Magistrate Randy Coffey on the grounds that Indiana's revenge porn law violated the right to freedom of speech. Coffey would state that he used guidance from the Minnesota appeal case to rule Indiana's law, unconstitutional.

Similar to Minnesota is the overturn of Texas' nonconsensual pornography law. On September 1st, 2015, the state made it a class A misdemeanor to publicly post intimate photos of a partner that were sent with the understanding they remain private. A violation of the law could bring a $4,000 fine and a sentence of one-year imprisonment. Texas' law was ruled unconstitutional in 2018 for being overly broad as it could be used to punish anyone that shared an image online regardless of if they knew the image was nonconsensual pornography. In 2019 however, the Texas Senate sought to fix the law, voting 31-0 to approve House Bill 98. The bill specifies that photos and videos must be posted with the intent to harm the person depicted and the offender knew that the victim had a reasonable expectation that the material would remain private. The bill was signed by Governor Greg Abbott and went into effect September 1st, 2019, providing other states a blueprint on how to re-write their own laws when faced with First Amendment challenges.

Currently there isn't a Federal law forbidding nonconsensual pornography, however an effort to make nonconsensual pornography a federal offense was introduced in 2017. Senators Kamala Harris, Richard Burr, and Amy Klobuchar introduced H.R.4472. Titled the ENOUGH Act (Ending Nonconsensual Online User Graphic Harassment), this bipartisan bill seeks to amend the federal criminal code to make it a crime to knowingly distribute (or intentionally threaten to distribute) an intimate visual depiction of an individual with knowledge of or reckless disregard for the individual's lack of consent, reasonable expectation of privacy, and potential harm; and without a reasonable belief that such distribution touches a matter of public concern. As of this writing, the bill sits in the House's subcommittee on crime, terrorism, homeland security, and investigations.

For Your Eyes Only

A common tone-deaf response to the victims of nonconsensual porn is telling them if they don't want their nude photos shared, they shouldn't take nude photos in the first place. But as writer and producer Lena Dunham states, that response is the equivalent of telling a rape victim that they should not have been wearing a short skirt.

The distribution of nonconsensual pornography, be it for clout or revenge, is a sex-based crime. For its victims, it carries the potential for emotional and mental damage, and can threaten professional and financial standings as well. And while state laws are a great response, a sweeping Federal law will potentially close legal loopholes, hold those who share private moments accountable, and send a National message about the seriousness of this crime. Melissa agrees, saying she is in favor of a Federal law like the ENOUGH Act passing.

"If anything, it will legitimize revenge porn as the form of sexual assault it is."

[1] Names have been changed to protect the privacy of the students in this case.

[2] Massachusetts, Mississippi, South Carolina, and Wyoming are the four states without laws that cover nonconsensual pornography.

7

—·—

FRUIT OF THE POISONOUS TREE: HOW TOXIC MASCULINITY PRODUCES SEXUAL ASSAULT

Poison Tree, Poison Fruit

P oison Tree, Poison Fruit

In the legal world, there exists a doctrine called the "fruit of the poisonous tree." Used as a rule to exclude ill-gotten evidence from court hearings, the metaphor claims if the source- or the "tree"- of evidence is tainted, then anything gained- the "fruit"- is tainted as well. This image of a decrepit rotting tree, high atop a hill, with its suspicious looking fruit hanging within arm's reach, also serves as a wonderful metaphor for toxic masculinity. Let's call it, the "Toxic Masculinitree."

The Toxic Masculinitree bares numerous fruit. Racism, domestic violence, general violence, homophobia, transphobia, and sexual assault all hang as products of the negative attitudes adopted to protect the male ego. And if these byproducts are the fruit, then dominion is the sunlight allowing them to grow on the vine. After all, it is the need for control that pushes the ego into negative areas. Racism is the thought that one race is superior to others. Domestic violence is the dominion of a spouse or partner using physical, emotional, or economic weapons. And sexual assault is the control over a person using sexual activity.

While you probably do not need me to define things such as rape, sodomy, or sexual abuse, it is important to look at these acts to see where dominion turns sex into a crime. Though part of the reason I studied law was to escape the mathematics requirement of other majors, the sexual assault equations are easy to grasp:

Sexual Activity + Consent = Positive Sexual Encounter

Sexual Activity - Consent= Sexual Assault

And it is the second equation where dominion meets its nasty cousin: entitlement.

The Soil

If dominion is the sunlight that allows the Toxic Masculinitree to grow, then entitlement is the soil, rich in nutrients, that strengthens the roots. It is that initial thought that as men, we are somehow owed something due to our penis, that makes way for the use of dominion to claim our target. When dominion and entitlement combine, the fruit of sexual assault blossoms on the Toxic Masculinitree. And once harvested, this fruit leads to the sex crimes we hear about, both on amplified mediums such as the evening news as well as in hushed tones from those close to us.

For an example of entitlement and dominion at work, take look at the Incel Community. The Southern Poverty Law Center currently describes the Incel Community as "part of the online male supremist ecosystem." It is listed alongside other hate groups dining on the fruit of the poisonous tree such as the Ku Klux Klan, Neo Nazis, and Neo Confederates.

The Incel community hasn't always been as nefarious as they are today. The earliest online use of the term "Involuntary Celibate" can be traced back to the year 1993 and a Canadian woman identified by her first name only, Alana. Curious why she, as an undergraduate at Carleton University, had never had sex or even a boyfriend, Alana created an all text website called "Alana's Involuntary Celibacy Project." The website's purpose was meant to be a supportive and inclusive community for men and women who, like Alana, were lonely and unlucky at love. And that is exactly what her Incel group was: a friendly community of lonely hearts, connecting to one another and providing each other support as they navigated through the romantic jungle. A few years after founding her website, Alana would discover her bisexuality, begin dating both men and women, and ultimately move away from the site, turning it over to a "man she didn't know." Years later, Alana would be horrified at what her supportive community had become.

Today, incel communities exist all throughout the internet. Gone is the supportive community and in its place is a cesspool of misogyny, sexism, and men who feel owed sexual relationships. Instead of taking personal responsibility for their romantic situation and seeking betterment, the modern day incel is fueled by entitlement which leads them to blame women for not succumbing to their physical desires. The modern incel views women as objects and openly expresses anger for his lack of sexual control over them. In many cases, incels will openly fantasize about committing acts of sexual violence against women, even calling for their rape as a means to obtain some perverse form justice against these women who have the audacity to not want to have sex with them. The combination of entitlement and dominion (in this case, the lack of) are the elements that keep the roots of toxic masculinity strong in this once supportive online community.

Planters of the Seed, Pruners of the Branch

While understanding Toxic Masculinitree photosynthesis is important, it is also crucial to know how these trees get planted in the first place. Typically, a culture of toxic masculinity is generational. In fraternities and sports teams, it is culture that is passed down from generation to generation, rarely questioned and largely accepted. Baylor University found the public spotlight on their football program in 2017 when a woman sued the university, alleging she was gang raped by members of the football team in 2013. Her lawsuit described a "Show 'Em a Good Time" culture of sexual violence the school fostered for years, which included taking underaged recruits to strip clubs and arranging for women to have sex with prospective recruits.

Meanwhile in Kentucky, 2015 would uncover a sex scandal at the University of Louisville where it would come to light that the Director of Basketball operations hired a self-proclaimed madam to provide women to dance for and have sex with players and recruits of the men's basketball team for a four year period. This would lead to the team being forced to vacate their 2013 National Championship. Both Baylor and UofL stand as examples of a long standing Toxic Masculinitree being systematically planted and pruned for years by authority figures in their respective athletic programs, and never being questioned by the student athletes that dined of its fruit of sexual objectification.

The same can be said in the family structure as well. The son does as his father before him, as his father before him. In 2016, Dan Turner's son was on trial for three counts of felony sexual assault that took place when he was a college student. Dan's son was convicted on all three counts. When it came time for sentencing, Dan read a letter out loud, begging for mercy for his son. The most outrageous portion of Dan's letter stated:

"His life will never be the one that he dreamed about and worked so hard to achieve. That's a steep price to pay for 20 minutes of action out of his 20 plus years of life."

Three felony counts of sexual assault for digitally penetrating a passed-out woman (Chanel Miller) behind a dumpster, reduced to "20 minutes of action." If this is how the father minimizes and views sexual assault, then it is no surprise that the son, Brock Turner, would include sexual assault in his masculinity profile. The Turners are just another example of the patriarchy hard at work — using the branches of toxic masculinity to prod its members into the laws and traditions needed to maintain the status quo of control. And part of that control, of course, is using women's bodies for sexual pleasure.

Be it a family setting or organizational student activities, Toxic Masculitrees are typically planted by elder authority figures and maintained by senior members throughout the years. The world of psychology shows us the tools used to allow these trees to stand strong. Operant conditioning is defined as using reinforcements and punishments to teach a desired behavior. Likewise, observational learning is described as the process of learning through watching others, retaining information, and replicating the observed behavior. Both are present in organizational and family constructs.

Younger members of social organizations and family units observe the behavior of older members of the group and take note of what behavior is rewarded in contrast to behavior that is punished. Rewards can include awarding arbitrary points or even membership itself to those who engage in desired behavior. On the other end, punishment often includes the public shaming of members who do not conform to the desired behavior of the group. Through observing the operant conditioning used to continue the organization's culture, members find themselves with only three options: leave the group, endure the ridicule, or fall in line. And, for a lot of these young men, fitting in, being liked, objectifying women as a bonding tool, and avoiding the insults of their peers is a much easier life than the alternative.

Excavation

So how does one go about removing a Toxic Masculinitree? Simple: cut it down. But what is the process of doing so? I have a tree in my yard that loses branches every so often and one day, a storm had knocked down a sizable branch right in my front yard. Realizing I could use said branch in my backyard firepit, I purchased a hatchet from Lowes. I had never cut wood before and was under the impression that it would be an easy process, requiring only a few hacks. What I quickly realized was that chopping wood is a much more difficult procedure. It requires numerous swings of the ax and is often a tiring process. And it certainly requires more than a small hatchet. After watching my struggle for about twenty minutes, a neighbor mercifully came to my aid and helped break the branch down.

Just as breaking down actual trees is a difficult task, so is chopping down a Toxic Masculinitree. You can attempt to do so yourself, but just like me in my front yard, you will realize that this a daunting solo task. It is a task that will leave one tired and often dejected. It is a task that could very well lead you to giving up because success will come very slowly, if at all. Instead, just as my neighbor gave an assist, Toxic Masculinitree excavation is more practical as a team project. And various men are doing just that: teaming up to strike it down.

Here are a few examples. The group A Call to Men rallies together to spark conversations about healthy and respectful manhood with men in positions ranging from professional athletes to members

of the Department of Justice. Fraternities at California Polytechnic
State University team up annually to produce an entire week of events
designed to educate men in the Greek system on what it means to
practice healthy masculinity in their groups. The players and coaches
of the Willamette University Men's basketball team, work to foster
a culture of healthy masculinity that not only grows their players as
athletes but also as human beings. The site Woke Daddy has created and nurtures a community for fathers to challenge the concep-
tion of masculinity and support one another in personal development. The #HeForShe movement builds upon the fantastic work of
#MeToo by inviting men across the globe to stand together in soli-
darity with women and encouraging allyship in the fight for gender
equality. All in all, men are working together in numerous venues to
chop down Toxic Masculinitrees. And as a result of their collabora-
tion, the wood is chipping and cultures are changing.

Once a Toxic Masculinitree has been uprooted, the soil will be ripe
for a new tree to be planted; a tree that bears the fruit of compassion,
respect, accountability, and consent. And this will be the fruit that
nurtures and grows those who eat it.

8

— . —

THE NEW NEW NINE: TITLE IX CHANGES THROUGH TWO VASTLY DIFFERENT ADMINISTRATIONS

S ince its enactment in 1972, Title IX of the Education Amendments, has prohibited discrimination on the basis of sex in any federally funded education program or activity. While the law was to address sexual discrimination across the board, it became popular as a law to enforce equality in athletics. Title IX was used to ensure women's sports teams received the same (or at least a similar) experience as their male counterparts. This included equality in equipment, facilities, and number of gendered teams offered.

Title IX would become so synonymous with athletics, that a 2011 Dear Colleague letter was written to remind practitioners that the law was to *also* cover discrimination and harassment in other parts of the educational institution as well. Specifically, the 2011 Dear Colleague letter discussed a campus' obligation to respond to sexual assault and sexual violence. This included both reporting and investigative measures for schools to follow.

Under the Obama Administration, Title IX would evolve to include protections for transgendered students as well. This progress would be especially helpful as the country was deep in conflict over transgender rights including their place in sports as well as which restroom one should use.

Then in 2016, Donald Trump became the President of the United States.

The Trump Era

A large part of the 45th President's legacy is his hatred for his predecessor, Barack Obama. Pre-White House Donald Trump was one of the loudest voices promoting birther conspiracies regarding Obama. Even after winning the Presidency, Trump couldn't help but to continue to insult and criticize the former President. With such distain, many were not shocked when President Trump would seek to undo many of the policies that President Obama would enact during his eight years in office, from foreign policy to environmental issues, and of course, Obamacare. It would also come as no surprise that the Trump Administration would seek to undo Obama's work in Title IX as well.

In 2017, United States Education Secretary Betsy DeVos announced that she planned to end the Obama Administration's rules for investigating sexual misconduct cases on campus, stating that they "failed many students and did a disservice to everyone involved." In September of that year, DeVos would rescind the Dear College letter stating that while it was well intentioned, it deprived the due process rights of many students; both the accused and the victims. DeVos would also announce her plans to overhaul the Obama Era Title IX policies, claiming that the previous administration had "weaponized the Office of Civil Rights to work against schools and against students."

On May 6, 2020, The Department of Education's (the Department) Final Rule arrived via a 2,033-page document. The reaction to the new regulations were divided. The Department stressed that the modifications "balanced the scales of justice on college campuses." Assistant Secretary of the Office of Civil Rights, Kenneth Marcus, stated that the rule sought to serve students on either side of a sexual misconduct complaint "marking the end of the false dichotomy of either protecting survivors, while ignoring due process, or protecting the accused, while disregarding sexual misconduct." Marcus continued, stating "there is no reason why educators cannot protect all of their students, and under this regulation there will be no excuses for failing to do so."

Meanwhile, criticism of the new regulations was plentiful as well. Critics argued that under the new regulations. universities would be "held less accountable for the actions of its students or faculty, cases may drag out as schools will not be held to the previous 60-day maximum to adjudicate cases, and victims of sexual violence may have to relive their trauma during cross-examination." The general consensus of criticism was that the new regulations made it more difficult to hold perpetrators of sexual harassment responsible for their actions, as the new reporting process had become more arduous under the regulations.

Colleges and universities were required to comply with the new regulations by August 14, 2020, leaving Title IX coordinators throughout the country to scramble to analyze the entire 2,033 pages of the regulation document, attend digital webinars and trainings, and prepare their campuses for the new procedures in the approaching fall semester. The new regulations contained many changes, but there were three that stood out as the largest and most monumental modifications to the Title IX legislation.

From Mandatory Reporters to Officials with Authority

106.44 (a) General response to sexual harassment. A recipient with actual knowledge of sexual harassment in an education program or activity of the recipient against a person in the United States, must respond promptly in a manner that is not deliberately indifferent.

Most universities make use of mandatory reporters; a system where the majority of university officials are required to report incidents of sexual misconduct to the Title IX office as they are made aware of them. While colleges adapted mandatory reporter policies to provide greater transparency in regards to the sexual assault statistics on their campus as well as their institutions accountability towards victims, critics worried that the new policies would have a negative effect on reporting. Critics of mandatory reporting policies stressed that students may be hesitant to do come forward, knowing that doing so would result in an official report being filed, without their permission. The Department agreed with this position stating:

> "The Department believes that respecting a complainant's autonomy is an important, desirable goal and that allowing complainants to discuss or disclose a sexual harassment experience with employees of postsecondary institutions without such confidential conversations automatically triggering the involvement of the recipient's Title IX office, will give complainants in postsecondary institutions greater control and autonomy over the reporting process."

As such, rather than utilizing mandatory reporters (or "responsible employees" as they are termed in the regulations), the new regulations stated that notice to the Title IX Coordinator or any other official with authority conveys actual knowledge to the institution. The regulations allowed universities and colleges to decide which of their staff and faculty must report sexual harassment to the institution's Title IX Coordinator. Institutions could still use a broad set of employees to report, including all employees if they wish. However, for the "actual knowledge" standard to be met, the person reporting must've been one designated as an official with authority.

Critics of this regulation pointed out that often, institutions discourage sexual harassment reports as the alleged perpetrators are often prominent members of campus communities such as athletes and fraternity members, among others. It was argued that by failing to make employees mandatory reporters, schools would be able to continue to ignore certain cases of sexual harassment, leading to fewer complaints and ultimately less justice for victims.

Commentators also pointed out that this regulation required victims to bear the responsibility of locating the correct administrator to report to, thus making it more difficult for victims to know how to properly report instances of harassment.

Title IX Jurisdiction

106.45(b)(3)(i) The recipient must investigate the allegations in a formal complaint. If the conduct alleged in the formal complaint would:

Not constitute sexual harassment as defined in § 106.30 even if proved,

Did not occur in the recipient's education program or activity, or

Did not occur against a person in the United States,

then the recipient must dismiss the formal complaint with regard to that conduct for purposes of sexual harassment under Title IX or this part; such a dismissal does not preclude action under another provision of the recipient's code of conduct.

Per the Trump Regulations, Title IX complaints that happened off-campus or not as part of a school program or activity were to be dismissed. In addition, Title IX complaints that happened outside of the United States must also to be dismissed. Supporters of this regulation stated that it imposed reasonable limits on the school's responsibility as well as addressing the unrealistic expectations of the school regulating student behavior in off-campus locations such as private apartments, frat houses and bars.

Opponents of this regulation were quick to point out that under this section, sexual assaults, harassment, intimate partner violence, and stalking that happen during study abroad programs or in off-campus housing, are not covered under Title IX. As 84.4% percent of students live off campus and rates of assault are approximately five times higher in study abroad programs, opponents argued that this regulation change was nonsensical. A 2013 study, based on 218 female undergraduate students at a single institution, highlighted the frequency of sexual misconduct in study abroad programs. The study showed sixty of the respondents (27.5 percent) reported at least one experience of unwanted touching while abroad, 13 (6 percent) reported an attempted sexual assault (anal, oral or vaginal), and 10 (4.6 percent) reported rape. Other statistics show that only 8% of sexual assaults take place on school property. Sexual assault prevention advocates worried that with such a low number of incidents transpiring on campus, the new regulation allowed for institutions to largely ignore the majority of sexual assault incidents that occur.

The Department responded that despite this regulation change, institutions would retain the flexibility to employ supportive measures in response to allegations of conduct that did not fall under Title IX's purview, as well as to investigate such conduct under the institution's own code of conduct at the school's discretion. The Department claimed it did not intend to dictate how an institution responded with respect to conduct that does not meet the conditions specified in § 106.44(a).

Live Hearings and Cross Examination

Section 106.45(b)(6)(i) Postsecondary institution recipients must provide live hearing with cross-examination.

Section 106.45(b)(6)(i) of the regulations, addressed the use of live disciplinary hearings in cases of sexual harassment. While a number of institutions make use of student conduct hearing boards to adjudicate violations of student policy, section 106.45(b)(6)(i) made live hearings mandatory. Live hearings often resemble judicial hearings with both complainant and respondent having the ability to issue statements, bring forth evidence, call and question witnesses, cross examine the opposite party and witnesses, and issue closing statements. Hearing board members are permitted to ask follow-up questions of all parties and ultimately determine if the respondent is responsible or non-responsible for the charged violation.

Commentators opine that requiring live hearings with cross-examination is the most important addition to ensure the regulations provide a fair process for all students involved. Supporters point out that cross-examination is "an essential pillar of fair process", necessary for resolving factual disputes in cases and is in line with Supreme Court cases interpreting due process of the law.

Critics stated that the new regulation allows for survivors to be cross-examined by their rapists' parents, friends, fraternity brothers or sorority sisters, thus greatly increasing the risk of re-traumatization. Meanwhile, others pointed to possible inequities in student legal representation. Title IX experts worried about unequal access to legal representation, pointing out the "huge asymmetry between male responding parties who can afford lawyers and female reporting parties who can't." Experts also anticipated the creation of a powerful incentive not to report for victims facing high paid lawyers and knowing they can't afford good legal advice of their own.

***

Despite due process supporters and survivor advocates finding themselves on rivaling sides of the Trump regulations, the policies took effect on August 14, 2020.

The Biden Era

After an extended vote count, denied motions to stop said counting, a handful of baseless claims of fraud, and an insurrection, on January 20th, 2021, Joe Biden dethroned the divisive and twice impeached incumbent to become the 46th President of the United States of America.

President Biden himself, is no stranger to the world of sexual assault prevention. During his time in the Senate, he would introduce the Violence Against Women Act (VAWA). Before VAWA was enacted, domestic abusers could avoid prosecution by crossing state lines and police were generally told not to intervene in domestic violence matters.

Appalled by the nation's lackadaisical attitude toward violence against women and marital rape, Biden would co-author the bill, putting in place a list of legal remedies to protect women from violence. Some of those remedies would include the Federal prosecution of domestic violence and sexual assault crimes that crossed state lines, as well as requiring states to enforce protective orders from other states. The act would be signed into law in 1994, with Biden calling it his proudest moment from his career in the Senate.

During his time as Vice President, Biden along with President Obama, aggressively expanded Title IX's reach from gender equality issues in sports to include sexual assault and the rights of transgender students. In 2011, the Office of Civil Rights issued their famous Dear Colleague letter. The letter would outline procedures and official departmental guidance under the law, telling school administrators at the collegiate and K-12 level that they were responsible for protecting students from sexual violence. The letter would also outline specific rules and procedures for how to handle claims of assault. Valerie Jarret, a senior advisor to President Obama, called the Dear Colleague letter historic, stating "while Title IX had always protected students from sexual harassment, this was the first time any federal administration called sexual violence a civil rights issue."

President Obama and Vice President Biden also launched It's On Us, a national campaign aimed at ending sexual assault. The campaign became known for inspiring events such as trauma informed yoga sessions and open mic nights at various college campuses. Over 440,000 people have signed the It's On Us pledge to commit to creating a culture of consent, bystander intervention, and survivor support. The initiative's reach has been felt at NCAA tournaments and the Academy Awards, with numerous celebrities and companies stepping forward in support.

In May 2016, the Obama Administration, citing Title IX, advised schools and colleges nationwide that they were required to allow transgendered students to access the restroom consistent with the gender they identified with. The guidance was a clear and direct response to educators, parents, and students asking for guidance under Title IX on how schools were to treat transgendered students in. The Obama Administration issued a 25-page document outlining policy suggestions alongside another Dear Colleague letter which made it clear that "under Title IX, a school must treat students consistent with their gender identity even if their education records or identification documents indicate a different sex." This directive was seen as a huge victory for transgender students and civil rights nationwide.

A Campaign Promise

While on the presidential campaign trail, Biden made it clear he intended to end the 2020 Title IX regulations which he claimed aimed to shame and silence survivors. There was, however, nothing quick about this process. Several anticipated dates for the Biden regulations came and went. By early April of 2024, Title IX coordinators and advocates, questioned whether Biden would deliver, at all, with the new regulations. Considering that 2024 was an election year and Biden was running against the still popular Donald Trump, it was a possibility that we'd might be stuck with the 2020 regulations for another four years.

But then without warning, the 2024 regulations were released early in the morning on April 19th, 2024. Coming in at 1,561 pages, the Biden regulations sought to strengthen protections, especially for the LGBTQ+, as well as to roll back some of the regulations made by the previous administration.

The Definition of "Complaints" and "Complainants"

Section 106.2: The Department therefore has modified the proposed definition of a Title IX "complaint" to be an oral or written communication to the recipient that objectively can be understood as a request for the recipient to investigate and make a determination about alleged sex discrimination under Title IX and the relevant implementing regulations.

With respect to a complaint brought by a former student or employee who was participating or attempting to participate in the recipient's education program or activity at the time of the alleged sex discrimination, the recipient should proceed just as it would with all other complaints under the recipient's grievance procedures in accordance with § 106.45, and if applicable § 106.46. If, at the time the complaint is filed, however, the respondent is no longer participating in the recipient's education program or activity or is no longer employed by the recipient, the complaint may be dismissed under § 106.45(d)(1)(ii).

Previously, if one wished to file an official Title IX complaint, the complaint had to be in writing and signed by the complainant. This had to occur before any type of formal investigation could start or any informal resolution could be offered. Opposers to this rule argued that the formal complaint requirement was arbitrary, overly prescriptive, and has the ability to allow an institution to ignore valid complaints that failed to conform exactly to the specific complaint requirements. Others noted that because of the fear of retaliation due to the level of detail required, postsecondary students are hesitant to submit formal complaints.

Supporters of the written complaint requirement stated that the process required the complainant to show a level of deliberation and informed action, which includes considering the consequences of filing a complainant.

Biden's regulations overturn the 2020 regulations by allowing oral complaints to carry just as much weight as a written complaint. In addition, The Department stated that a complainant need not use any particular "magic words" to trigger a university's obligation to investigate the matter.

Section 106.2 also addresses complainants who were discriminated against while enrolled in or employed at a university, but have since left. The 2020 amendments required complainants to either be participating or attempting to participate in the university's education program or a university activity at the time of filing a complaint rather than at the time of the alleged discrimination.

Of course, victims of sexual misconduct often hesitate to report for a multitude of reasons, sometimes opting to leave an institution to get away from the hostile and threatening environment. The 2020 regulations left survivors who took this route, no recourse. As The Department noted, this regulation made it more difficult for universities to investigate, address, and stop sexual harassment, as it forced them to dismiss Title IX complaints brought by prospective students, former students, and former employees who experienced sexual harassment while affiliated with the university.

Thus, section 106.2 expanded the definition of a complainant to include former students and employees who were affiliated with the university at the time of their discrimination. The section calls for the university to "proceed just as it would with all other complaints under the recipient's grievance procedures."

One thing that didn't change under this section was the procedure for respondents who have already left the university when a complaint is filed. If the respondent is gone, then he is out of the university's jurisdiction and as such, the complaint may be dismissed. This allows respondents to avoid responsibility by changing institutions, often times without the new institutions being aware of the complaint filed at the former.

Title IX Jurisdiction

Section 106.11: The Department has deleted the reference to "even if sex-based harassment" from § 106.11 and replaced it with "even when some conduct alleged to be" in final § 106.11 to clarify that a recipient has an obligation to address a sex-based hostile environment under its education program or activity in the United States, even when some conduct alleged to be contributing to the hostile environment occurred outside the recipient's education program or activity or outside the United States.

One of the more controversial changes in the Trump regulations was the geographical limitations of the university's responsibilities under Title IX. Sexual misconduct was required to physically happen on campus in order to fall under the purview of Title IX. This removed protections for those assaulted in an off campus fraternity house, at an away sporting event, or in an private house.

Supporters of overturning this section highlighted that doing so would "better reflect where sex-based harassment occurs given that students live, learn, and participate in 195 education programs off campus and in remote settings." Others noted the many student populations that would gain protections, including graduate, vocational, and community college students; low-income students, students of color, former foster youth, and LGBTQI+ students, student athletes, and students who attend training and workforce development programs. Furthermore, supporters noted that section 106.11 would close the gap created by the Trump regulations that essentially allowed respondents to engage in off campus misconduct and avoid disciplinary consequence.

Section 106.11 then, creates an obligation for schools to respond to misconduct that happens outside of the school's programming and outside of the United States as well. This means that sexual misconduct that happens on university study abroad trips are now back under Title IX's jurisdiction. Amending this regulation now allows institutions to address sexual misconduct where it is *actually* happening.

Live Hearings and Cross Examination

Section 106.46(f)(g): The Department has determined that the requirements in the final

regulations at § 106.46(g) for the live hearing process, and § 106.46 (f) for the live-questioning

process if a postsecondary institution chooses not to use a live hearing, appropriately protect the

right of all parties to have a meaningful opportunity to present and respond to allegations of sex-based harassment.

Whereas the 2020 regulations made live hearings mandatory, this was consistently met with criticism, due to the possibility of re-traumatizing the victim, with commentators noting that removing the live hearing requirement would cause less trauma for complainants without impacting parties' due process rights. Other commentators noted that mandatory live hearings chill reporting, as victims are hesitant to come forward out of fear of a lengthy and embarrassing hearing process.

Other commentators make the argument of whether mandatory hearings are practical for smaller institutions as they place an undue burden on the institution to find the manpower to coordinate these hearings. They argue that making live hearings optional "will enable smaller postsecondary institutions to pursue alternatives to live hearings that encourage reporting and address fears of retaliation."

Supporters of the 2020 requirements continue to point to due process as the primary reason to require live hearings. Others, championing the rights of the accused, state that there must be balance with the rights of the accuser, and identify the live hearing as the necessary tool to do just that.

Instead of the complete elimination of live hearings, the 2024 regulations do not require a mandatory live hearing as long as the institution provides an alternate option for live question asking. These options could range from one-on-one sessions with the parties and the adjudicator, where prepared questions are asked. This could also include the use of video conferencing software like Zoom (which some institutions already utilize). These options provide universities a level of discretion on how it wishes to adjudicate, allowing institution options to best serve trauma affected complainants. If a complainant expresses uncomfortableness facing the accused or fielding questions from them in a cross examination, universities now have more options to offer at their disposal.

Strengthened Protections for the LGBTQI+ Community

Section 106.10: Discrimination on the basis of sex includes discrimination on the basis of sex stereotypes, sex characteristics, pregnancy or related conditions, sexual orientation, and gender identity.

Commentators from over 40 states shared instances of discrimination, harassment, and bullying based on sexual orientation and gender identity. Both teachers and counselors shared experiences with providing support to students struggling with the effects of being bullied because of their sexual orientation and gender identity. LGBTQI+ students (and their parents and teachers) commented that harassment, bullying, and threats of physical violence leave this community of students in "constant fear, cause social anxiety and stress disorders, and too frequently result in suicidality."

Commentators against Title IX expanding its protections to include discrimination based on sexual orientation and gender identity chimed in with a variety of statements. Some opposing commentators stated that the proposed regulations would, "in their view, harm many cisgender women and their futures." Other opposing commentators "expressed general concern that the proposed regulations would, in their view, interfere in the personal lives of families." Others stated that cisgender students "experience discomfort at school when they are required to participate in activities and share facilities with transgender students." It should be noted that none of the opposing commentators provided any evidence, data, or case law to support their claims.

In the end, the Department decided to expand the regulations to provide protections for those experiencing discrimination based on both sexual orientation and gender identity. Despite this amendment, the Department notably silent on the long-standing debate of transgender students playing for sports teams corresponding to their gender identity.

August 1st, 2024

The Biden Era Regulations came with an implementation date of August 1st, 2024. This date allowed for the regulations to be prepared for the 2024 school year. It is the hope amongst advocates and Title IX coordinators alike, that no more sweeping change to the regulations are on the horizon. Tribalism in American politics remains at an all time high, with each party continuously looking to outdo the other. Sexual misconduct in education, however, should not be the battleground for this political warfare. Each academic year brings a new class of college students, paying always rising tuition to pursue their degrees. These students deserve stabilized protection from sexual misconduct to do so.

Let us hope that any further changes in the near future, only serve to build upon those protections, instead of taking them away.

9

— · —

WHAT I LEARNED ABOUT SEXUAL ASSAULT EDUCATION IN HIGHER EDUCATION FROM NASPA

M y law school education has led me down a rather unique professional path. While my fellow classmates dreamed of fighting all manner of legal battles in the courtroom, my legal journey led me to use my Juris Doctorate to compete with the other doctors of philosophy in the world of academia. Landing my first post law school job as the Director of Equity & Diversity and Title IX Coordinator at a four-year, state university, placed one of my feet in the legal world and the other in higher education; two professions where appearances are held in the highest of regard.

While attorneys take their carefully manicured headshots in front of a wall of never read Court Reporters, the world of higher education is one where the letters at the end of your name are often more important than your name itself and published journal articles act as high currency.

And then there are the conferences.

Presenting your research at an academic conference is one of those expected tasks for higher education practitioners looking to elevate their CV. It is considered a high honor to be chosen to fly out to a large city, check into the "conference block" of slightly discounted hotel rooms, and give an hour-long lecture to a room full of your colleagues. Given the numerous scholastic and professional areas in higher education, you can imagine there are a magnitude of conferences that welcome attendees throughout the country, annually. And perhaps the most prestigious of these conferences is the National Association of Student Personnel Administrators (NASPA) Conference. NASPA touts itself as the "premier student affairs professional development event" where thousands of participants engage with featured speakers who provide hundreds of thoughtful educational sessions.

In 2021, I submitted a proposal to NASPA for a session teaching professionals how to create a practical and engaging sexual assault prevention curriculum for fraternity men. The proposal began by outlining the barriers that normally prevent this population from fully engaging in this type of education. Professionals would then be provided tried and tested methods on how to address these barriers. Overall, the audience would learn that by providing education that has less to do with shaking an accusatory finger and instead, focusing on forming lasting relationships, universities will be able to create allies for the continued fight against collegiate sexual assault.

The proposal was denied.

By reading the critical comments left by the selection panel, I learned far more information about sexual assault education in colleges than I could by actually attending the conference. Specifically, I witnessed the stances and attitudes that still cause universities to miss the mark when it comes to providing practical and relatable sexual assault prevention education for their Greek men.

"Far more discussion of popular media coverage than research or theory."

Academics live by their academic research. Early in a student's college career, they are taught how to search the numerous academic journals available to them for research that serves as the foundation of their essays, term papers, and final assignments. On the PhD level, the last obstacle students tackle is producing a formal piece of research called a dissertation which includes a very specific research question and what other researchers have said about it. Doctoral students will endure their own data collection process and analysis, finally answering their original thesis question based on their rigorous research. In other disciplines like law school, much emphasis is placed on having your research published in a legal journal such as a law review, with the promise of an employer pleasing achievement dangling in the balance for those that do. As such, law review articles are packed with careful research including case law, statutes, and what other legal students have theorized on the same topic.

At the heart of academic research is the systematic explanation of a set of facts and laws, or the "theory". Given its foundational significance, theory is thought of as the source of one's research. It is the motivation that drives a specific research project and is one of the three main elements in the traditional model of the scientific method.

It can be agreed that research and theory are both important factors when presenting an idea or new method of doing something. And it is indisputable that academic journals and published dissertations are in fact, troves of scholarly knowledge. But to ignore popular media coverage and pop culture in research is a great oversight, especially when your target audience consumes this type of media in large quantities. A 2010 study from the Kaiser Family Institute, reported that students between the ages of 8 and 18 spent approximately 7.5 hours a day consuming pop culture through television, music and video games. Social media of course, is another channel in which Gen Z students intake pop culture with reports showing that students spend about three hours per day logged into sites like Instagram, Snapchat, and the addictive Tik Tok. With these levels of pop culture consumption and technology usage, it is no surprise the methods in which students prefer to be educated in, would shift as well. In a 2018 Pearson study, nearly 60% of Gen Z students reported a preference to learning from videos posted on YouTube versus learning through traditional means such as apps, textbooks, or group activities.

Simply put, understanding who your work is meant for, means understanding exactly what type of research will connect with them best. While empirical research may be what impresses the crowd at an academic conference, your typical 18 or 19-year-old freshmen likely has different interests.

As an educational tool, pop culture can be used to make concepts of sexual misconduct relatable to a younger audience. For example, consider the teaching of bystander intervention. Teaching students how the diffusion of responsibility effects group behavior, provides a good academic understanding of the bystander effect and makes substantial fodder for a five page essay on the subject. Analyzing the 2021 story of a woman being raped on a public train in Philadelphia while onlookers recorded the assault on their cell phones and refused to intervene however, provides a relatable educational center piece for discussion. Teachers can assign students to read the story, watch the CNN newsclip of the story, and then discuss times they have been in an uncomfortable public situation as a bystander.

As another example, consider a lesson plan centered on violence against women. Teaching students the statistic 35% of women world-wide have experienced either physical and/or sexual intimate partner violence or non-partner sexual violence prepares them for the semester's final exam. But telling the story of how iconic music producer Dr. Dre, assaulted reporter Dee Barnes by slamming her head into a brick wall and brutally kicking her in the ribs due to being upset over one of her articles, allows for a more interesting teaching of violence against women. It provides students with a well-known, public figure, which allows for the removal of some of the abstractness of violence against women. It also turns a statistic into a dynamic story which opens the door for compelling conversation.

In 1988, eventual rapper and actor Tupac Shakur, gave a now iconic interview about the disparities of the education system. In between calling for classes that would teach students about relevant issues such as police brutality and drugs (past the D.A.R.E. oversimplification of "just say no"), Tupac took sex education to task as well. Tupac said:

"There should be a class on sex education. No, a REAL sex education class, not just pictures and illogical terms."

Although this quote was only a small part of the interview, it is crucial as it provides a critique on the lack of relevance in the teaching of sex and by extension, sexual assault, in the school. Education steeped in empirical research, that parrots various theories and approaches may slay the crowd at an academic conference, full of professionals with a high level of education. It may even be of interest to an upper classman or graduate student when presented in a criminal justice or behavioral studies course. But for an 18- or 19-year-old college freshman, research and theory without an agent that makes this information pertinent to them, is largely irrelevant in preparing them for the real world.

"I don't think learning the unique barriers for fraternity men and approaching sexual violence prevention as an ally are really worth going to a session for. I think everybody at the conference already gets that."

To indicate that education about the barriers that prevent a student population, known for their incredibly high percentage of campus rapes, from learning about sexual assault prevention "is not worth going to a session for", is a bold declaration, considering that students themselves highlight universities consistently dropping the ball in this area. A 2014 study revealed that 43% of female students believe that their school is not doing enough to combat sexual assault on campus. Statistics such as this show that higher education practitioners may need to have a more open mind to different forms of education.

In my experience as a university Title IX coordinator, I can state that fraternity men usually encounter sexual assault prevention at two different points during their time as undergraduates. The first is during the university's orientation activities. When I attended my freshman orientation in 2001 at the University of Louisville, our student orientation leaders performed a variety of skits designed to approach topical student issues such as time management, learning how to make friends on campus, and substance abuse. Tucked in the middle of these skits was a 90 second act on sexual assault. No information on campus resources like the Title IX office or the student advocacy center was included. The act simply ended as the orientation leaders got into place for the next one on how to study in the library.

The problem with including sexual assault prevention into orientation activities is three-fold. First, orientation is a time where students are regularly overloaded with information. Between taking class placement exams, learning the physical lay of the campus, engaging with the many recognized student organizations all vying for new membership, and locating campus resources such as the library and writing centers, a freshman's bandwidth during orientation runs thin. It is questionable how much information the freshman will retain on this packed day. The day of orientation being crowded with information leads to the second issue with this method of education; schools are not able to dedicate much time to sexual assault prevention when there are other high priority topics that must be discussed. Spending minimal time on sexual consent, bystander intervention, and campus policy not only limits the amount of information that can be conveyed to students, but also sends a unconscious message about where sexual assault prevention falls on the universities pecking order of priorities. Lastly, sexual assault prevention at orientation hardly benefits eventual fraternity students as the education typically presented is of a general nature. As students have not yet committed to a fraternity at the point of orientation, general education makes more sense for a group of unaffiliated students. Students who do decide to go Greek however, will soon find themselves in a microcosm of campus life full of its own unique situations that require more than general education to navigate.

The second point where sexual assault prevention education is presented to fraternity men, comes in the form of punishment for already performed assaults. It is not uncommon to see fraternities engage in educational sessions after a chapter incident has become public and adjudicated by the student conduct process. In some cases, these education sessions are mandated by the university's judicial arm. Other times, a fraternity will preemptively arrange chapter education as a way of "falling on their sword." Regardless of which party coordinates this type of leaning, it is rarely received enthusiastically. Rather, it is more common for fraternity members approach this brand of education as an annoyance; a necessary evil required to eventually restore their chapter's standing in the campus community.

While wedging presentations in the middle of already crowded orientation programs, presenting education as a punishment, and requiring fraternity members to hurriedly click through online educational modules may do well in checking off boxes on a compliance checklist, research has shown that brief, introductory programs focused on awareness are not effective at changing attitudes and behaviors in the long-run. Instead, a more focused and comprehensive program is needed to focus on a group's specific environment and issues, making the training more relatable and the effect longer lasting. Take for example, The U.S. Naval Academy's Sexual Harassment and Assault Prevention Education (SHAPE) program. This four-year curriculum is designed specifically for midshipmen with the goal of guiding them through the peer education sessions, various seminars, and scenarios that mirror real-life situations that junior officers will face. SHAPE doesn't just check a box; it imbeds healthy sexual behavior in the academy's culture.

Earlier in this very book, I discuss at length the elements that make sexual assault prevention education a taboo topic for fraternities. Uncomfortable self-evaluation, organizational tradition, accusatory tones in teaching, and generational toxic masculinity, all act as barriers to educating fraternity men on sexual assault prevention. To understand these barriers is to understand your audience. And understanding your audience, allows educators to create targeted and practical education that will not only keep fraternity men engaged, but will lead to sexual assault education inspiring cultural change instead of being another box checking activity.

"Indicating that fraternity men are incapable of learning from those who do not identify with them seems to digress from a promising approach to intervention."

Perhaps the most authoritative word on practical methods to teach fraternity men about sexual assault prevention, comes from the audience itself. In November 2021, I was hired by the Interfraternity Council at Indiana University in Bloomington, Indiana, to do a half day of consulting work. At 9:00AM on a brisk Friday morning, several hundred fraternity men fought through the remaining haze of the previous night's social shenanigans to corral into a lecture hall in the university's business school. For four hours, I taught these young men how to build their own new member sexual assault education programs. We worked together to craft chapter mission statements for the fraternities to use as their north star when addressing sexual misconduct. Lastly, each of these men walked out of the room with a baseline knowledge of bystander intervention as I navigated them through the Green Dot certification process. While previous calls I had made to the university's Greek Life office to provide this exact same education had led to numerous unanswered emails and ignored voicemails, here I was guest lecturing in the Kelley School of Business at the request of the students themselves.

This half day was void of any complex terminology. The presentation of statistics was kept at a minimum. The tweed jacket with the leather patches was kept at home. Rather, I chose a hunter green L.L. Bean Snap Tee, jeans and a pair of Sperry Topsiders to match the casual aesthetic of the day. And from time to time, a little colorful language was sprinkled in as a tool of relatability. After the final lecture was given, several of the men hung back to express their gratitude and take a few pictures. One young man made a statement that showed his gratefulness in the way the information was presented. He said:

"It was so refreshing to have someone who understands us to come and speak about this stuff. This has been the best presentation we've ever had on this stuff and it's because you understand us and know the things we're going through."

This statement is reveals several things. First, it highlights that the university has attempted this type of education in the past. Perhaps it was the school's Title IX coordinator. Or maybe it was a speaker from the campus advocacy center. Regardless, someone has previously approached this audience before. The second thing this statement shows is that the level of unrelatability between these previous speakers and the students affected the delivery of the message. This is evident as the student placed an emphasis on the fact that it was my understanding of them that made this "the best presentation they've ever had" on sexual assault prevention.

To ignore the significance of being able to relate to students as an educator, flies directly in the face of research done to highlight the need of diverse faculty in the classroom. A 2017 study surveyed 80,000 public school students across six different states. The study found that when students had teachers of the same race as them, they reported feeling more cared for, more interested in their schoolwork, and more confident in their teachers' abilities to communicate with them.

Gender is another area where a student being able to identify with their teacher produces unique benefits. In a 2015 Texas A&M study, the analysis of the test scores of 14,000 South Korean middle school students, showed that when being taught by a woman, girl's test scores where almost 10% higher than the scores of the boys in the study. Female students in the study reported feeling that their female teachers are more likely to give students an equal chance and are more likely to encourage creative expression.

It must be noted that these studies do not state students of color and female students are incapable of learning from teachers of a different race of sex. It does however highlight the student's benefits gained by learning from a teacher they identify with. The same principle applies to those who teach students in Greek organizations. Theoretically, anyone can teach a fraternity the Green Dot curriculum, which provides a premade script and PowerPoint presentation for its trainers to follow. An instructor that has an audience he identifies with however, is able to infuse this lecture with relatable scenarios and common fraternity examples that the audience can see themselves in. He is also able to do this with a higher sense of authority than a lecturer who has not lived these examples themselves. Fraternity men are capable of learning from *anyone*. But when the lesson comes from someone they identify with, as the kids say, it hits different.

The Purpose of it All

If a university's goal is to better fraternity culture by including heathy sexual behavior as a priority, administrators must approach new methods of education with an open mind. Administrators must refrain from shying away from seminars that don't match the research templates they were taught in their PhD level classes and understand the importance of relatability with the audience they seek to effect.

As for the presenters wishing to change the culture with new and innovative workshops, while conferences like NASPA may stand tall as the industry standard for presenting and exchanging research, it is important to consider some of the lesser-known conferences that will put you directly in front of your desired audience. Conferences like the ones hosted by Southeast Greeks , the Association of Fraternal Leadership & Values, and the North American Interfraternity Conference, allow presenters not only the opportunity to present their research, but to present it to the audience that will benefit from it the most.

10

—·—

COSBY, KELLY, AND RACIAL INJUSTICE IN
SEXUAL ASSAULT CASES

The Tarnished Media Maven

Bill Cosby's career began in the 1960's and spanned six decades through stand-up comedy, television, film, and music. With a career covering so many areas through such a large duration of time, your age will indicate which Cosby you're most familiar with. In her sixties at the time of this writing, my mother still recalls Cosby's comedy performances on specials such as 1968's *To Russel, My Brother Whom I Slept With* and 1983's *Bill Cosby: Himself*. In my late thirties, I vaguely remember watching Fat Albert as a child. I greatly recall however, going to the theater to see such films as *Ghost Dad* and the universally-panned *Leonard Part 6*. And who could forget watching Dr. Cliff Huxtable and family dance to "Kiss Me" each week on NBC's *The Cosby Show*. For many young Black children in the 1990's, their first interaction with college was checking in on the weekly happenings at Hillman College, the fictional HBCU in the Cosby produced show, *A Different World*. And of course, there were the memorable JELL-O Pudding ads which featured the comedian for almost 30 years. In the Black community, Bill Cosby was in very rare air. He occupied a space reserved for only the most excellent in our community. A space filled with other luminaries such as Oprah Winfrey and Michael Jackson. Bill Cosby was more than an icon; he was a *Black* icon.

As a result of Cosby's iconic stature, when he was formally charged in 2015 with three counts of aggravated indecent assault, the Black community took it especially hard. It's not as if allegations of sexual assault were new for Cosby. For as long as his career has spanned, so has the allegations of sexual misconduct, including rape and drug facilitated sexual assault. For decades however, fans and colleagues alike willfully turned a blind eye to these allegations. It would not be until 2018 that Cosby would finally be held to the law and found guilty for sexual misconduct that happened 14 years prior.

In a 2005 deposition, Cosby admitted to buying Quaaludes (a sedative and hypnotic medication) from gynecologist Leroy Amar for the purpose of giving them to women he wanted to have sex with. Cosby's testimony would ultimately show a history of coerced sex involving Quaaludes with multiple young women. Cosby would also admit that he knew giving the drugs to others was illegal. Despite being initially sealed, the contents of this deposition would play a role in Cosby's eventual undoing in 2018, when he was found guilty of three second degree felony counts of aggravated indecent assault against Andrea Constand, an employee of Temple University.

The Pied Piper of R&B

While not on the same level of success as Cosby, Robert Kelly is yet another fallen Black icon, buried under years of sexual misconduct accusations. Kelly's career began in 1989 as a member of the R&B group Public Announcement. In 1993, he would leave the group and embark on a solo career that lasted three decades. During that time, Kelly would sell over 75 million records, placing him at the top of the list of R&B male artists in the 1990's and gaining him the nickname, the King of R&B. In addition to R&B, Kelly would also successfully dabble in gospel and was a mainstay in the hip hop world, collaborating with some of the most successful artists of the genre including The Notorious B.I.G., T.I. and Jay Z.

As with Cosby, Kelly's history of sexual misconduct was not necessarily a secret. In 1994, a then 27-year-old Kelly married fellow singer Aaliyah; a controversial union considering Aaliyah was only 15 at the time. Kelly would even produce Aaliyah's debut album; the boastfully titled, "Age Ain't Nothing But a Number." Then in 2002, R. Kelly's legal troubles would begin. At the time, he was preparing to release his first joint album with rapper Jay Z as well as his monumental *Chocolate Factory* album. It would also be the year that a Chicago newspaper received an anonymous delivery of a videotape that allegedly depicted R. Kelly engaged in sexual intercourse with an underage girl. The "*R. Kelly Sextape*" would be sold at swap meets and barbershops throughout the country; never mind the fact it was child pornography.

Kelly would not stand trial until 2008 where he was charged with 14 counts of child pornography. At trial, the prosecution needed to prove that (1) R. Kelly was the man in the tape, (2) the girl on the tape was underage and (3) the tape was genuine. R. Kelly's defense claimed that the singer has a distinctive mole on his back and as the man in the tape did not have the mole, it could not have been Kelly on the tape. When it was pointed out that you in fact could see the mole, the defense claimed the marking was a video artifact and not the mole that Kelly has.

The largest element in Kelly's favor however, was the girl's unwillingness to testify. Stephanie Edwards (a singer formerly signed to R. Kelly's label) would testify that the girl in the tape was her niece and was in fact, underage. Kelly's defense would respond saying that Edward's testimony was a measure of revenge on Kelly for dropping her from his label, further casting doubt in the jury's mind. So, despite the video showing Kelly's face and being filmed in a room on a property Kelly owned, the jury found the singer not guilty on all charges.

Kelly's musical career would continue following this trial. Then in January of 2019, the documentary *Surviving R. Kelly* premiered on the Lifetime channel. Over six episodes, the documentary detailed Kelly's long history of sexual misconduct with under aged girls. As a result of the docuseries and a more politically correct climate, Kelly was dropped from his longtime recording label RCA, had his music removed from numerous radio stations, and had numerous musical colleagues denounce him.

In February 2019, a new sex tape emerged depicting an alleged R. Kelly involved in sex acts with a 14-year-old girl. At the time of this article, R. Kelly is awaiting his trial for 18 federal charges including child pornography, kidnapping, and various sex crimes.

Why us and not them?

The fall of Kelly and Cosby produced a very curious response. While most condemned both men for their heinous actions, a loud voice in the Black community spoke in a more supportive tone. Rather than condemnation, the argument was made that both Bill Cosby and R. Kelly were victims of strategic character assassination and that their convictions were a plot to destroy Black masculinity. Many asked what the point of charging both men for crimes that happened "so long ago" was. Others questioned whether the misconduct even happened, indicating that the accusers were only coming forward for financial gain. At the height of the argument was a widely shared meme, featuring the headshots of white celebrities such as Charlie Sheen, Bill O'Reilly, Harvey Weinstein, and Donald Trump. The question asked;

why has "justice" been served to these two Black men but not these white men of similar stature? The fix was in and the media was attacking the Black community by tearing down their most successful leaders.

Now, anyone that takes the five minutes of research required to actually be informed on the matter, will be able to quickly see the issue with the meme. Not every case of sexual misconduct is equal. At the time of the meme's sharing, Harvey Weinstein had only been charged and had yet to go through the legal system (*Author's Note*: Since the original writing of this article, Weinstein has in fact received numerous convictions and years of imprisonment). Charlie Sheen's accuser had passed away several years earlier and no charges were filed. Bill O'Reilly committed sexual harassment (not a criminal offense) and had settled his lawsuits for millions of dollars. And Donald Trump hid behind his presidency, boldly reminding the country that a sitting president cannot be charged with a crime (*Author's Note*: Since the original writing of this article, Donald Trump was found liable for the sexual abuse of E. Jean Carroll). Despite these individual cases however, some continue to live by the time-honored, social media philosophy, "never let facts get in the way of a good narrative."

To say that Black men have historically been given a tough time in court would be a huge understatement. Black men are more likely to receive tougher sentences for their crimes than others and are also imprisoned at six times the rate of white men. Other research shows that nearly 1 in 12 Black men, aged 25–54 are incarcerated, compared to 1 in 60 nonblack men, 1 in 200 Black women and 1 in 500 non-Black women. Research from the group ThinkProcess shows that in many of the country's largest cities, Black men are more likely to be treated as criminals, which includes being stopped and frisked by police more often than any other group. And one need not have to look too hard to find numerous cases throughout history that highlight the unfair treatment of Black men in the judicial system; from the Central Park 5 (more on them later) to the Trenton 6 (six Black men who were arrested for the killing of a store owner and, despite all having rock-solid alibis and not matching the description of the actual killers, were coerced into confessions, found guilty by an all-white jury, and sentenced to death (later overturned on appeal)).

So yes, the argument that Black men are unfairly treated in the judicial system is a valid one that most certainly should be made. But should Bill Cosby and R. Kelly be the champions of this fight? In the words of *The Boondocks'* fictional 10-year-old revolutionary, Huey Freeman:

"Yes, the government conspires to put a lot of innocent Black men in jail on fallacious charges, but R. Kelly is not one of those men!"

And for the simple matter of guilt, neither is Bill Cosby.

Our True Champions for Racial Injustice

Though some may argue that R. Kelly has yet to be convicted (*Authors Note*: Kelly was convicted in 2021) and thus it is unfair to write him off just yet, there are still much cleaner choices one can select when arguing that Black men are unfairly treated in sexual assault cases. When selecting a champion for the cause of racial justice in sexual assault cases, the prerequisite should be unequivocal innocence. Unfortunately, the American justice system gives us many options to choose from. Five viable champions for this argument are Kevin Richardson, Antron McCray, Yusef Salaam, Korey Wise, and Raymond Santana: otherwise known as the Central Park Five. In 1989 these five boys, aged 14–16, were convicted of the rape of a white jogger in Central Park. The case drew much criticism due to the false confessions that were coerced from the boys. The boys served between six and seven years apiece, except for Wise who was tried as an adult, serving 13 years. In 2002, the charges of all five boys would be vacated after the true rapist confessed from jail. The Central Park Five's story was recently retold in the Netflix miniseries, *When They See Us*.

There is also the case of the Groveland Four who, in 1949, were accused of raping a 17-year-old white girl, tortured into confessions, and convicted by an all-white jury. In 2019, they would all receive pardons for the wrongful convictions. Unfortunately, all four of them are dead; Samuel Shepherd was shot by a sheriff who transported him to a retrial, Ernest Thomas was killed by a mob shortly after the incident, and Charles Greenlee and Walter Irvin both served life sentences.

If you would rather go solo than do the group thing, there is always Archie Williams who in 1982, was convicted of attempted murder and rape in Louisiana. Now keep in mind, three people testified that Williams was at home asleep when the rape occurred, the fingerprints at the scene did not match Williams' and the sole witness did not point out Williams in two photo line ups. Despite all this evidence, Williams was still found guilty and sentenced to life without the possibility of parole. The wrongful conviction would not be vacated until 2019.

You could also cite the case of South Florida's Barney Brown. In 1962, 15-year-old Brown was accused of raping a woman and robbing her husband. Due to the woman's inconsistent and contradictory story that failed to positively identify Brown as the culprit, the teen was acquitted in juvenile court. But a silly little acquittal would not stand in the District Attorney's way. Brown was charged again, this time in an adult criminal court, and the DA got the guilty verdict he was searching for. It would take 38 years for Brown's conviction to be overturned under double jeopardy laws, making it unconstitutional for a person to be tried again after being acquitted for the same crime.

Of course, if you are looking for something even more "historical", there's always Emmitt Till. In 1955, Till was accused of whistling at a white shop owner, Carolyn Bryant. Till was kidnapped, beaten, and ultimately lynched by Bryant's husband Roy and his half-brother, J.W. Milam. While Till never saw the inside of a courtroom, his killers did. But as this was the Jim Crow South, it only took about an hour for an all-white male jury to find both Bryant and Milam not guilty. Five decades later, after the deaths of Till, Roy, J.W. and the entire Civil Rights Movement, Carolyn Bryant would come forth to admit that the most damning parts of her testimony (that Emmitt grabbed her hand and waist) were lies. It should be noted that despite her admission, Bryant has never faced any amount of justice for her role in Till's murder.

These names are just a few of many; the many who have had years of their lives stolen by a justice system that has tortured and tormented to get confessions, ignored evidence, and wrote off alibis on the journey to convict their Black targets. It is no surprise that racial minorities make up the vast majority of those assisted by the Innocence Project, which, since its founding in 1992, has been working tirelessly to exonerate the wrongly convicted through DNA testing.

While the names I've listed above may not be as glamorous as those of media barons and R&B kings, these names are the ones that actually make the point that when it comes to sexual assault in America, Black men have been historically railroaded by the system. Next time you wish to make that point on Facebook, skip the Cosby/Weinstein comparison and choose the Central Park 5/Brock Turner one instead.

11

---·---

POLITICIANS SAY THE DARNDEST THINGS

P oliticians exist in an environment where sound bites and posturing are common currency. And as such, the ground is ripe for these public servants to make as many if not more head scratching statements about sexual assault as their legal counterparts. Often desperate, commonly offensive, and always cringe-worthy, here are some of the darndest things politicians have said about sexual assault.

Forensic Findings

We begin deep in the heart of Texas where everything is bigger, including the gaffes that come from politician's mouths. As I've said numerous times before, anytime someone goes on a crusade against women's rights, a cringe worthy comment is right around the corner. This was true in 2013 as Texas law makers labored over a restrictive anti-abortion bill. When an exemption was proposed for women who were rape victims, State Representative and sponsor of the bill, Jodie Laubenberg, claimed such an exemption was unnecessary due to rape kits. Laubenberg stated that, "in the emergency room they have what's called rape kits, where a woman can get cleaned out."

After receiving a hearty round of mocking for her statement, Laubenberg would claim that she had been confused by the Democrat who was asking her questions and misspoke. To most however, it was clear that Laubenberg's true confusion was about the exact purpose and utilization of rape kits.

In the 1970's there was no standard method to collect forensic evidence. There also was a lack of understanding of the psychological effects of sexual assault. Therefore, if a woman didn't appear especially traumatized following an assault, her case was often times dismissed. Enter Martha Goodard, a sexual assault survivor who interviewed numerous medical, legal, and law enforcement experts on a mission to find a uniform way to collect this evidence that would be crucial for convictions. Through her friendship with Hugh Hefner's daughter Christie, the Playboy Foundation provided the initial funding for the kits. The kit itself was developed by Louis Vitullo and consists of a container that includes a checklist, materials, and instructions for whoever is overseeing the procedure. It also includes envelopes and containers to package any specimens collected during the exam. The first kit was utilized in 1978 in an Illinois hospital and today are widely available.[1]

You would think the chair of the House Committee on Public Health in Texas, would have a base understanding that a forensic exam and abortion are not the same thing. But of course, you would be wrong. Laubenberg would end her career in the Texas house, retiring in 2019.

Worse Than Rape

Next, we go to 2016 with Kentucky's Senate Bill 150 which set out to include local law enforcement as persons authorized to collect DNA samples. The bill also aimed to allow for the collection of DNA samples at arrest or initial appearance from all persons charged with a felony offense. As with any bill that is before Senate consideration, there is a period of testimony for either support or opposition of the bill in question. In expressing his opposition, then Majority Caucus Leader Senator Dan Seum stated, "I can tell you, and I understand your pain, but I can tell you, and I have eight children and twenty-one grandkids that, over the years, this government through its intrusion has done more damage to me than any of these criminals out there ever did." Keep in mind this statement was uttered in a hearing that included testimony from a mother whose daughter was raped, murdered, and set on fire by her attacker.

In August of 2003, Katie Sepich was out with her friends celebrating the beginning of grad school at New Mexico University. After getting into an argument with her boyfriend, she stormed off and by the time her friends awoke the next morning, she was nowhere to be found. After a morning of calling hospitals, jailhouses, and frantically searching for Katie, her remains were found near a local landfill. She had been sexually assaulted, strangled, and in an attempt to destroy the evidence, burned. A DNA sample found under Katie's nails led authorities a year later to Gabriel Avila. Avila had been in prison since November 2004 and while there, finally submitted a DNA sample that matched the DNA taken from Katie.

Katie's mother Jayann is credited with working on what would be called, Katie's Law. At the time of her daughter's death, DNA would be taken only after someone was convicted of a crime. Under Katie's Law, DNA would be taken at the time of arrest for a felony. Had Katie's Law been in effect at the time Katie Sepich was murdered, her killer would have been caught within months of his crime. The law would be passed in 2006. In 2008, Jayaan Sepich and her husband David, founded DNA Saves, a nonprofit organization committed to working with every state to pass laws to expand the DNA database and fund DNA programs. As of 2020, 25 states have passed Katie's Law, or an equivalent.

Politicians (and humans in general) have long been criticized for not caring about issues that don't affect them. Despite Seum claiming he understands the pain of someone effected by sexual assault, his comment certainly does not reflect empathy with the matter. Fortunately for him, he was able to shed the burdening trauma of government overreach when he retired from the State Senate in 2019. But even Seum himself would thumb his nose at our final subject.

Parting Gift

Staying in the Bluegrass State, we end with the former Governor of the great commonwealth, Matt Bevin. Who knew that waging war against the state's teachers wouldn't be a wise campaign strategy? But in November 2019, Bevin found himself defeated and on a one-way ticket out of Frankfort. While an outgoing governor handing out pardons is a common practice, it is a bit eyebrow raising to see convicted murderers and hitman employers on the list. Equally as alarming is the inclusion of convicted child rapists such as Kenton County's Micah Schoettle. In 2018, Schoettle was found guilty of the rape, sodomy, and sexual abuse of a young girl, with the assault beginning when the girl was just nine years old. While he was sentenced to 23 years imprisonment, he would only serve 18 months after receiving a pardon from the outgoing governor. When asked how he could pardon a convicted child rapist, Bevin would respond by saying "which one?" And while that statement alone deserves its own article, Bevin's comments about Schoettle's victim is what lands him here. Bevin stated that he based his pardon on the fact the young girl's "hymen was still intact." The former Governor would continue saying, "this is perhaps more specific than people would want but trust me. If you have been repeatedly sexually violated as a small child by an adult, there are going to be repercussions of that physically and medically."

Using an intact hymen as evidence of sexual activity is not an uncommon mistake for a layperson. In 2019, rapper and entrepreneur T.I. drew many justified claims of misogyny when he revealed that he regularly takes his 18-year-old daughter (an adult that is certainly able to make her own decisions about sex) to the gynecologist to make sure her hymen and thus, her virginity is still intact. While that may fly in the Harris household, one would think the standard for pardoning a crime befitting a 23-year prison sentence would be a bit higher than layperson opinion.

Just as they are utilized in the courtroom, expert opinions are a very helpful tool at an elected official's disposal in helping to explain issues on a scientific, technical, or specialized level. Regarding using the state of the hymen to prove sexual assault, Dr. Caitlin Thomas, an OBGYN resident in Indiana, states the following:

"I know it's not surprising to you, but I believe that the former Governor doesn't know what he is talking about. Testing for an intact hymen is not a proper or valid way to test for rape. Just as a transected hymen cannot be used to confirm prior sexual activity, the presence of an intact hymen cannot confirm no sexual activity. The hymen is a ring of mucous membrane surrounding the introitus, or opening, of the vagina. Sexual intercourse can happen without a tearing of the hymen and cannot be used to rule out penetrative sexual assault. Though it may not have been relevant to this specific case, it is very important to note that sexual assault can occur without penetrative vaginal intercourse."

Expert opinions are not difficult to obtain and should be utilized when a decision maker lacks factual knowledge on a decision they are making, such as releasing a convicted child molester back into society with little punishment and no rehabilitation. However, when you are on a salt the Earth farewell tour that includes pardoning the crimes of people who have financially supported your past campaigns, perhaps expert opinions aren't your number one priority.

Conclusion

Medical experts play a variety of roles. In addition to serving the health needs of the general public, they typically know a great deal about their field. Whether it is understanding the utilization of DNA in sexual assault cases or bathing a layperson opinion in a scientific light, medical experts are here to help. All it takes is the calming of the ego and a simple ask to avoid saying one of the darndest things about sexual assault.

Or freeing a convicted child molester.

[1] Despite the availability of rape kits, backlogging is a major problem. Tens of thousands of rape kits go untested with states seeking legislation to combat the issue.

12

— • —

HOW BAD DO YOU WANT IN?

F all Rush, 2001

For me, fraternity recruitment began with an event called Rho Alpha night. A Rho Alpha is an active member of a fraternity that deactivates for the week of rush to act as a guide to potential new members. And on this Sunday evening, they would guide us to visit each of our university's 11 fraternities. Each group would be stationed in a classroom or auditorium on campus, and we would spend 15 minutes as the members would try to convince us that their house was the best.

At this point, my only knowledge about Greek Life came from movies like Animal House and Road Trip as well as the handful of fraternity parties I wandered into over the summer. I knew about the free-flowing drinks. I knew about the jaw droppingly gorgeous sorority women. And I also knew about the hazing.

It is not like hazing was some sort of big secret. Through warnings from my mom and the fraternity stories on the big screen, I knew you did not just walk into a brotherhood. But in my little 19-year-old freshman brain, I wrote these potentially life-threatening actions off as no big deal. Yeah, they might make me drink alcohol. But boozing it up was one of the main reasons I was joining a fraternity in the first place. And sure, they might try to do things like making me streak the quad to embarrass me. But I was a theatre kid and as such, hadn't been embarrassed since 4th grade. A little light pestering in exchange for the life-long brotherhood that was promised would certainly be a fair exchange.

What *did* worry me however, was the physically violent hazing. I knew what those wooden paddles hanging from the frat house wall were for. I also knew that some of the black fraternities had a propensity for heating up Greek letter shaped pieces of metal for the purpose of searing each other's flesh. And then there was the sexual stuff. It was always rumored what some fraternities made their pledges do to each other or what the older brothers would do to them.

But those were just rumors.

I mean, they didn't *really* do those things.

Right?

I tried to put these horrors out of my head as we went from room to room for the fraternities to try and impress us. And try they did! Some boasted having the best grades on campus while others showed us pictures of the ski trips and beach getaways their chapters took. One house even had their overly hair gelled president take the stage to tell us an asinine story of how when their chapter walks in the local bar, every guy gives them their seat, their beer, and their women. This was all fine and entertaining, but the vibe in the Sigma Alpha Epsilon (SAE) room was much different.

When we got to SAE, all of us prospective members sat at individual desks in the middle of the room. The active members meanwhile, surrounded us by standing next to each other against the classroom wall; dressed in their finest clothes and staring at us in distain. While the chapter president bragged about their vast collection of intramural sports trophies, I could not stop starring at one brother standing in the front of the room. He stood about 6'3 and was around 200 pounds of lean muscle. He wore a dress shirt like the others, but his had the sleeves removed to show off his muscular arms, adorned with all different matter of tattoos. Think peak level 50 Cent, wearing a repp stripe tie instead of his spinning G-Unit chain. As I watched him, I thought about what hazing might be like at the hands of Mr. Olympus. I thought about the velocity behind his paddle swings and... hell no.

Nope.

SAE was out of the question.

The last house we visited was Tau Kappa Epsilon (TKE). If SAE was about intimidating precision, then TKE was about the exact opposite. In place of the pristinely pressed button downs were red and green rush shirts, reeking of the prior night's cigarette smoke and spilled beer. And while they had a few members that you could qualify as "in shape", there were no Mr. Olympuses present. The thought that I could hold my own against any of these guys if the hazing got out of hand, put my mind at ease about the house I would eventually call home.

"We Have a Strict No Hazing Policy"

The above is a typical phrase that can be found in many university student conduct policies and handbooks. It is a phrase that scores of fraternity men utter to prospective members when they are courting them for membership. Despite these policies, hazing remains an issue in a variety of male centered organizations. Reports show that 1.5 million high school students are hazed each year with 25% being hazed before the age of 13. On the collegiate level, over 250,000 student athletes report being subjected to hazing activities while 73% of members in Greek organizations have experienced some form of hazing.

It would appear these organizations did not receive the "no hazing policy" memo.

Intended to be a method to embarrass, humiliate, and emasculate its victims, hazing comes in many forms. Dartmouth College produces a hazing checklist that includes subtle hazing acts, such as isolating new members, depriving new members of rights that would normally be afforded to other members, and name calling. The college defines harassment hazing as making new members wear humiliating attire, depriving them of sleep, and subjecting them to verbal threats. Included in the violent hazing category is the act of branding, paddling, water intoxication, forced alcohol and drug consumption, and expected abuse of animals. While these acts are crimes in themselves, hazing also ventures into the area of sexual assault.

Acts that fall in the category of sexual abuse hazing include everything from verbal sexual humiliation to sodomy. And while this form of hazing may be underreported due to the embarrassment its victims may feel, it happens on a quite regular basis. In 2017, the Associated Press examined sexual violence in school sports and found approximately 17,000 official reports of sexual assaults by students in the grades K-12 over a four-year period. A year prior in 2016, the United States Army reported that male hazing was its most common form of sexual assault. And while we don't have comprehensive data on sexual abuse hazing on the collegiate level, the internet is rife with stories of frat house horrors and locker room sodomy.

Sexual abuse hazing makes a clear and common statement about masculinity. Perpetrators use this form of hazing to weaponize[1] same-sex sexual interaction in order to feminize and homosexualize their victims with the purpose of establishing their position at the bottom of the organization's power structure. Sex abuse hazing in male groups re-enforces the toxic generalization that homosexuality does not fit into society's profile of masculinity and gives its practitioners a way to excuse sexual assault and sexual harassment.

Pennalism and Fagging

It is commonly accepted that hazing got its beginning in 387 B.C. with the founding of Plato's Academy in Greece. Plato himself would describe the practice, then known as pennalism, as "practical jokes played by unruly young men that injured the hazed and citizens who got in the way." He would go on to describe the perpetrators as "wild animals." Pennalism would continue into the Middle Ages and would include acts such as forcing freshmen to wear odd clothing, as well as subjecting them to extortion, verbal harassment, and physical abuse.[2]

In the 16th century, British public schools utilized a system called fagging as a method to maintain discipline among male students. Junior students would be required to act as servants for the older boys. Tasks would include shoe shining, cleaning clothes, and cooking meals, amongst other jobs.

1636 would see the opening of the first American college, Harvard University. Practices similar to fagging were practiced at Harvard, likely being brought by students who had their previous education in England. A list from the 1856 book, *A Collection of College Words and Customs*, provides insight to the scrutiny freshman at Harvard endured in the 1700s. Freshmen were forbidden from laughing at their senior classmates, asking their seniors any "impertinent" questions, intruding in their seniors company, or wear their cap in their senior's chamber. Freshmen were expected to complete errands "hastily" and during sporting events, were expected to retrieve any "bats, balls, or footballs" their seniors may be using. Item 21 on the list calls for the severe punishment of any freshman that broke any of the customs.

The end of the American Civil War, saw returning soldiers bringing a more military, bootcamp flair to hazing practices, including beat-
ings, the force feeding of vile substances, and faux kidnappings. 1873
would see the first recorded hazing death when Mortimer Marcellus
Leggett was blindfold and forced to walk alongside a railroad tres-
tle with other pledges of Cornell University's Kappa Alpha Society.
Leggett would strike the back of his head, leading to his death. While
Leggett's death would be the first, it certainly would not be the last due
to hazing. In the many years since Leggett's death, physical violence,
dangerous drinking games, and mentally debilitating humiliation tactics have awaited thousands of boys and men looking for entrance or
acceptance in various social organizations.

Sexual Abuse Hazing

Author and psychologist, Dr. Susan Lipkins, is a leading authority
in campus conflict and violence in high schools and colleges. She states
that sexual abuse hazing is a more modern invention, tracing practices
back to the 1990's. In the Greek world, sexual hazing typically takes a
less violent form, more concerned with the humiliation of members.
Verbal abuse such as calling pledges "ladies" or "fags" serve the purpose
of emasculation while other methods of hazing are utilized. Other
forms of sexual hazing include making new members dress in women's
clothing to designate pledges as less than men. A 2012 investigation
of Salisbury University's Sigma Alpha Epsilon chapter show both
practices in use. A university report from one of the brothers allege
that brothers forced new members into a dark basement and made
them stand with their backs against the wall. Once lined up, brothers
hurled homophobic insults at the pledges, saying they would be made
to "suck a dick" and calling them "good for nothing faggots." On

another occasion, pledges were made to wear dresses and high heels while older members paddled them.

The elephant walk is a hazing activity that requires pledges to strip naked and stand in a line, holding the penis of the member behind them. The pledges are then forced to walk around in a circle. Some variations of the act require the pledges to stick their thumb in the anus of the person in front of them. The practice has long been rumored a part of hazing activities, yet rarely confirmed. But in 2017, text messages exchanged by members of Penn State's Beta Theta Pi Fraternity seem to indicate the chapter had in fact used this form of hazing on their members. The chapter was under investigation for the hazing death of one of their pledges when text exchanges captured the president saying "if ever there was a time to do an elephant walk, it would be tonight."

This is not to say that fraternities don't use physical sexual abuse in hazing practices. In a 2011 lawsuit against UC Davis, a former pledge of Jewish fraternity Alpha Epsilon Pi, claimed he was sexually abused during an initiation event. Ryan Clifford claimed he was subjected to the fraternity's harshest form of hazing called "ratfucking", due to him being the only non-Jewish member of his pledge class. During a mandatory trip to lake Tahoe, members forced Clifford to strip naked and then fondled his penis while making sexually demeaning comments. In 2018, the Texas Christian University chapter of Delta Tau Delta was shut down due to hazing allegations. Brothers of the chapter locked their pledges in a closet and forced them to simulate sex with blow up dolls and use sex toys on one another.

If the physical sexual abuse in fraternity hazing could be considered "light", then the sexual hazing in the sports world is downright brutal. In 2012, two new members of the Andover High School Basketball team participated in a hazing ritual known as "Ookie Cookie." The game (also known as "wet biscuit") requires members to masturbate at the same time and ejaculate on a piece of food. The last person to ejaculate must then eat the food. The Andover incident was captured on the camera phone of one of the teammates. Turning to the more violent side of sexual hazing, in 2017, La Vernia High School in La Vernia, Texas came under fire when a Federal lawsuit exposed a culture of sexually violent hazing in its sports teams. The report detailed one student who had to endure hazing in his advancement from the junior varsity to the varsity football team. The 15-year-old was held face down on the locker room floor while another student pushed a Gatorade bottle into his anus. In his sophomore year, varsity players would continue the hazing by fondling him and pushing a cardboard tube up his anus as other teammates cheered.

In 2018, five boys from the Damascus High School Football team in Maryland faced rape charges for a hazing incident that happened on Halloween. The boys turned out the lights in the locker room and pinned one of their victims to the floor. Once down, the boys held his feet, repeatedly punched him and violently sodomized him with a broom handle in a hazing ritual called "brooming." A second team-mate was also pinned to a bench and sodomized with the broomstick. Two other boys were attacked but were able to fight their attackers off before they could be violated themselves. An investigation uncovered that "brooming" had been a part of the team's freshmen hazing rituals since 2016.

A investigative story from ESPN shows that sodomy has become the hazing activity of choice in youth athletic teams with more than 40 incidents happening between 2011 and 2016, the year the report was released. Dr. Lipkins states that kids have become more desensitized to sexuality and see this form of violent sexual hazing as a way to humiliate others. And while this is true, the attacks are not just limited to juveniles.

In 2020 the Penn State football team, an athletic program with a history of sexual misconduct, made the news due to a sexual hazing incident. Former player Isiah Humphries filed a Federal lawsuit against the university claiming various acts of sexual hazing. Humphries alleged that older players would pin their younger teammates on the floor, climb on top of them, and hump them. He also stated that older players would rub their genitals on the faces and buttocks of the younger players as well fondling their genitals. To add insult to injury, younger players were regularly told by their older teammates that they were going to "Sandusky them"; a threat invoking the name of former Penn State assistant coach Jerry Sandusky who was convicted of 45 counts of child molestation.

A similar incident was reported in 2023 involving the Northwestern University football team. On July 8, 2023, The Daily Northwestern newspaper released the details of the incident. The team used a practice called "running" to embarrass and punish players who made mistakes during practice. Players selected for running would be restrained by eight to 10 of their teammates dressed in various "Purge-Like" masks. The player would then be "dry humped" in a dark locker room by the older players in a scene described by a player as a display of "absolutely egregious and vile and inhumane behavior." When a player was selected to be "ran," teammates would clap their hands above their heads while surrounding the player in question. This became known as the "Shrek Clap". The article states that "running" was especially common during the holiday season with a white board in the locker room having the words "Runsgiving" and "Runsmas" scrawled across it and the names of players who had been selected for running underneath.

Another tradition of sexual misconduct practiced by the team was called "The Car Wash". Here, players would stand naked at the entrance to the showers and spin around, forcing those entering the showers to rub up against their nude bodies. Players even set up a hose connected to the shower to spray people which one player described as "extremely painful."

The junior hockey leagues in Canada have also been home to some of the most demeaning sexual hazing in athletics. From the 1980s to 2001, Canadian Fred Ledlin was something of a journeyman hockey player, playing for more than 10 junior professional teams in his career. Ledlin would describe the sexual hazing he endured in several detailed affidavits filed in Canadian court in 2020. Ledlin states that while playing for the Victoria Cougars in the 1980-1981 season, the end of a hockey stick was forcibly inserted in his anus by older players. The team veterans also dipped a pin in liquid heat and then inserted the pin in Ledlin's urethra. The next season Ledlin played for the Kamloops Junior Oilers, where new members were taped to hockey sticks until they were unable to move their arms and legs. Older members would then tie the lace from a skate to the rookie's penis, throw the lace over a venting pipe, then tie the other end to the handle of a bucket. The bucket would then be weighed down with hockey pucks, pulling the player's penis. Ledlin would recall 49 pucks being placed in the bucket during his round of the excruciating practice. Elsewhere in the affidavit, another athlete who played in the Ontario Hockey League in the 1990s described a hazing tactic called "mashing" where rookies were required to eat the chocolate pudding out of the buttocks of the older members.

Outside of Greek and Jock life, the Military serves as another breeding ground for sexual hazing. Specialist Jarrett Wright came forward to tell his story of sexual hazing that occurred in 2010 when he was deployed in Iraq. Wright recalled being thrown onto a bed by several sergeants who pinned his shoulders down with their knees. Once subdued, the sergeants fondled Wright's genitals and sodomized him with their fingers. Wright states he was familiar with this type of attack as it had previously happened to his roommate. A 2015 report from the Government Accountability Office (the investigative arm of congress) described a hazing activity where soldiers would throw objects at the crotch of their victims, telling them hazing would only stop if oral sex was performed on the assailants. Then in 2017, Navy Seal Tony DeDolph and Marine Mario Madera-Rodriquez devised a plan to embarrass Army Staff Sergeant Logan Melgar for a perceived slight on their unit. As described by the prosecutors assigned to the case, Melgar was to be rendered unconscious through the use of a choke hold. Once out, the Sergeant was to be molested while the attack was videotaped. The hazing attempt went fatally wrong as Melgar died of strangulation while in the chokehold.

Whether on the humiliating side or on the violent end of the spectrum, it is clear that male organizations that use sexual hazing, view same sex interactions as the antithesis of what is considered "manly" or masculine. And for a practice that's purpose is to emasculate, sexual hazing serves as the perfect tool.

Media Portrayal

For those fortunate enough to have never experienced sexual hazing firsthand, mainstream media has routinely portrayed real life practices in a variety of films and television shows. Often played for laughs, sexual hazing has been included in numerous fraternity-centric movies. In 2001's *Going Greek*, pledges were led into a basement and forced to play a game of Ookie Cookie as a part of their hazing. Upon completion of the game, the losing pledge comically vomits. The 2008 comedy *College* focuses on three high school seniors that stay at a fraternity house while on a weekend campus visit. The brothers of the house haze the boys by sending them to a gay fraternity's party as a prank. Later, the boys are made to drink alcohol off the body of one of the brothers, including liquor that was poured down the older member's buttocks and into the boy's mouth. In 2017's *Frat Star*, pledges are routinely subjected to verbal abuse, being referred to as "sperm chuggers," "faggots," and other homophobic slurs.

In the more serious and surreal categories, during a season two episode of the Donald Glover helmed show *Atlanta*, the protagonists find themselves smoking weed on a fraternity house couch after fleeing from a fight at a campus concert. The principals watch in horror as a group of fully nude pledges with burlap sacks on their heads are forced to dance to the song Laffy Taffy while standing in formation. In a scene from a season nine episode of *American Horror Story*, pledges from the show's Omega Xi fraternity are shown doing an elephant walk with an older brother instructing them to "grab a cock, trunks to tail." The death and sodomy of a fraternity member was the central plot of a season five episode of *Law & Order: Special Victims Unit* entitled "Brotherhood." In the episode, a violin bow was the weapon of choice used to sodomize the victim.

If mainstream media makes mention of sexual hazing through its inclusion in film and television, then the adult film industry has turned it into its own subgenre. With content dating back to 2011, the website Fraternity X claims to follow the exploits of a real fraternity from a university in Arizona that created a gay pornographic site to "put themselves through college."[3] The site claims that the brothers consider themselves straight as they have "plenty of girls and bitches to bang on the side", and that they only have sex with each other for money. Scenes depicting sexual hazing are scattered throughout the site with clear descriptions of what viewers can expect. Take for example the description of the site's February 21st, 2021 upload:

"This skater boy has been hanging around the frat for days, begging to become a pledge even though it isn't pledge week. So, we cut the little bitch a deal. If he can handle all of the brothers, we'll let him in."

Or this description from the July 1st, 2020 video entitled "Pledge Train":

"If you want to join our frat, gotta [sic] contribute to the house. We had to break it down for this new pledge. Every guy not in our group is a bitch and we all know what happens to bitches. So, to initiate him in, we all lined up for the train and made him a bro. Flooded that bro hoe hole."

The descriptions make it clear for viewers that sexual hazing is a part of this fictional fraternity's pledge process. While hazing scenarios only make up a portion of Fraternity X's content, it is the central focus for the site Haze Him.[4] The site boasts being "the official site for straight fraternity guys getting hazed into gay sex." To add a more realistic element to their content, the site claims to offer a chance to win $10,000 to viewers who send them footage of their pledges doing "gay sex acts." With numerous videos being regularly updated, it appears that sexual hazing is big adult business.

The Law

The first anti hazing law was passed in New York in 1894 as a response to an incident at Cornell University where chlorine gas was released into the dining hall during the annual freshman banquet. The prank killed one staff member and injured numerous others. Since then, 44 states have adopted some form of anti-hazing legislation with some statutes being stronger than others. For example, at the time of this writing only 10 states make hazing a felony when it results in death or serious injury. Also, some states such as Kentucky, limit their laws to only govern members of a campus community leaving no anti-hazing reprieve for incidents that happen outside of an academic setting. At the time of this writing, there has not been any Federal legislation passed banning hazing. However, the Education Notification and Disclosure of Actions risking Loss of Life by (END ALL) Hazing Act, has been proposed. The Act would require institutions that participate in Federal student aid programs to collect information and publicly report hazing related misconduct. As of this writing, the bill is under review by the House Committee on Education and Labor, where it has sat since 2019.

Cases involving sexual hazing tend to become complex due to the number of legal realms these cases have the possibilities of venturing into. Of course, some cases do focus on the criminal aspect of sexual hazing. At a football training camp in 2008, several football players at Robertson High School in Las Vegas were victims of sexual hazing at the hands of their older teammates. Seven younger players were sodomized with broomsticks at the hands of older teammates. The older students told the victims to "take it like a man or it will get 10 times worse." The perpetrators would eventually plead guilty to criminal charges with the ringleader of the assault, Mark Gallegos, receiving the heaviest sentence after pleading guilty to two counts of criminal sexual penetration, three counts of attempted criminal sexual penetration, and one count of conspiracy. He served around 21 months in juvenile detention. In addition to the criminal suit, the seven victims also filed a civil complaint against the Las Vegas, N.M. School Board, various district superintendents, the high school's athletic director and football coaches, the owners of the football camp, and of course the perpetrators themselves. In 2011, a 5.25 million dollar settlement was reached.

As one would expect, sexual hazing in school settings also trigger Title IX claims. Brian Seamons[5] was a football player at Sky View High School in Utah. On October 11,1993, Seamons was pulled from the locker room shower by five of his upper-class teammates and forcibly stripped naked and restrained to a towel rack with adhesive tape. Once restrained, one of his teammates brought one of Seamons' ex-girlfriends into the locker room to view him. Seamons reported the incident to several school administrators including his coach, Douglas Snow. In response, Snow brought Bryan before the football team, accused him of betraying them, and ordered Bryan to apologize. When Bryan refused to do so, he was dismissed from the team and ultimately moved to a new school due to threats and harassment from fellow classmates. The interesting part of Seamon's case is that it raised no complaint of the original assault against him by his teammates. Rather, his Title IX claim focused on Snow's response, highlighting statements the coach told him such as "he should have taken it like a man" and that "boys will be boys." Seamons contended that through his response, the coach "expected him to conform to a macho male stereotype." Seamons's claim would fall short as he was unable to prove that the abuse he faced was sexual in nature.

While Seamon's case stood upon Title IX, sexual hazing in the workplace has the potential to prompt Title VII sexual discrimination claims. In 1998, Joseph Oncale[6] was an oil rig worker for Sundowner Offshore Services, Inc. Oncale was regularly subjected to humiliating, sex-related acts including being sodomized by a bar of soap. When the hazing was reported to Oncale's supervisors, no remedial action was taken and Oncale was called a homosexual slur. Oncale would eventually leave his job stating in his deposition that he felt if he did not leave, he would have been raped. Oncale's case would focus not on the criminal side of the hazing, but rather if the hazing violated Title VII; specifically, whether Oncale had been discriminated against because of his sex. After two years of legal wrangling, the Supreme Court found in favor of Oncale, stating that Title VII did protect him from the harassment he endured.

As the above cases show, there are many directions that sexual hazing incidents can go legally, from criminal charges to civil settlements. But while legislators mull over the strengthening of future statutes, it is important to understand the root of sexual hazing and its place in the masculinity profile.

A Toxic Statement

It comes as no surprise that practitioners of hazing would use sexual assault as one of their methods of abuse as the foundations of sexual assault and hazing are interchangeable. Like hazing, sexual assault is a practice in dominion as psychologists state that the motivation for sexual assault stems from the perpetrator's need for dominance and control. In many cases sexual assault arises in environments where there is an uneven power dynamic; the perpetrator being more dominant than the victim. This mirrors the environment that hazing thrives in. Due to their seniority, older members of an organization hold more social standing than the newer ones, and as such are more dominant than their pledges or rookies. Another way to examine this power dynamic is through the explanation of Alpha and Beta males. The Alpha male is considered as being on top of the social hierarchy. Using physical prowess and domination, he has gained power and success. Meanwhile, the traits of a Beta male include weakness, submissiveness, and subordination. Both sexual assault and hazing sees the Alpha exerting his control over the Beta.

The use of sexual assault to establish dominance is heavily practiced in prison culture. In prison, perpetrators target newly incarcerated inmates who are unfamiliar with prison culture and who appear to be less likely to fight back. If the new inmate is able to fight off and resist an assault, he is deemed a "man" and will be less likely to be a target for assault in the future. If the inmate is not able to fight off an attack, he will be labeled as "turned out." Once an inmate is turned out, it will be very difficult for him to regain his status as a man, and he will be targeted for future attacks. The mirroring of prison culture is not lost of those outside of confinement. In Isiah Humphries' lawsuit, he states that the upper classmen on his team intended "to make the new guys their bitch", telling them "this is prison." From the yard to the football field and the frat house, same sex sexual assault is used as a weapon to strip someone of his manhood and place him in a submissive role.

The desire for dominance is further established when looking at the consequences victims face when they resist their abusers. Fred Ledlin states the reason his teammates hazed him more than others is because he would fight back. His boldness would only lead to more humiliation from the veterans on the team. Dr. Lipkins agrees with this notion, stating in a 2015 Yahoo Health article, "if you protest the hazing, you will probably get hazed worse." However in other cases, perpetrators may all together bypass victims they think are likely to successfully resist in search of easier targets. In recalling sexual assault hazing he previously witnessed, former artillery soldier Edward stated that he was never subjected to it himself due to his size. Rather, the older soldiers in his unit focused on new soldiers who could not defend themselves against a group of attackers. This targeting is intentional; attack those who you know you will be able to achieve the goal of domination against.

Sexual assault in hazing is also a practice in masculinity; to prove your own, you must diminish the masculinity of another. And acts of sexual hazing emphasize the perception that same sex affection is on the weak end of the masculinity spectrum. This explains why sexual assault is the weapon of choice utilized in male-dominated environments. In a 2020 Government Accountability Office report, one military officer made the connection between the Military's hyper masculine culture and sexual assault:

"Military culture encourages men to see themselves as dominant males and leaders, and being sexually assaulted makes you feel like you are less than a man, helpless and weak."

In a 2014 GQ article, James Asbrand a psychologist with the Salt Lake City's VA's PTSD Clinical team, makes the statement that sums up the purpose of sexual assault in hazing:

"In a hypermasculine culture, what's the worst thing you can do to another man? Force him into what the culture perceives as a feminine role. Completely dominate and rape him."

Both comments show two important aspects of the relationship between sexual hazing and masculinity. First, it reiterates that in order for someone considered "a real man", they must have dominion over another. But secondly, it makes a statement on where homosexuality falls on the masculinity scale. Homosexuality was long been stereotyped as weak, with gay men being viewed as feminine, the opposite of their heterosexual counterparts. While the victims of sexual assault in hazing may not be gay themselves, their perpetrators force them to "play the role" in order to achieve their ultimate goal of demonstrating the "appropriate" masculine face. And while the perpetrators themselves are involved in these acts, it is important to remember that sexual assault is not about sex but rather, is about dominance. That principal outweighs the reality that attackers are participants in the exact behavior they have deemed as "less than."

Using proper and academic explanations, we tend to dance around the penultimate truth; sexual hazing is not hazing at all. While it may be done for humiliation and control purposes, lumping it under the umbrella of hazing only serves to normalize and diminish the crime as well as the effect it has on its victims. When the roles are changed and women are the victims of this same behavior, society has no problem referring to the perpetrators as rapists. Yet when it happens as part of hazing, statements such as "boys will be boys" are uttered by coaches, advisors, and even parents providing a way to write off the committing of a crime that perpetrated anywhere else, would draw the ire that these acts deserve. If we are to change this culture, we must treat these sexual assaults in hazing no different than we would treat any other sexual assault.

Violating a teammate anally with a broomstick is not an initiation ritual.

It is sodomy. A sex crime.

Calling a co-worker a faggot is not "boys being boys."

It is sexual harassment and in some states, an element of a hate crime.

Holding a fellow soldier down and forcing your genitals in his mouth is not horseplay.

It is sexual abuse.

And sexual hazing is not hazing.

It is sexual assault.

[1] Jeckell A.S., Copenhaver E.A., Diamond A.B. The spectrum of hazing and peer sexual abuse in sports: A current perspective. *Sports Health.* 2018;**10**:558–564. doi: 10.1177/1941738118797322.

[2] Brown, Tamara L.; Parks, Gregory; Phillips, Clarenda M. (2005). *African American Fraternities and Sororities: The Legacy and the Vision.* University Press of Kentucky.

[3] It has been routinely questioned whether Fraternity X is a real fraternity or not with most signs pointing no.

[4] There is also a sister site called Haze Her which features similar content featuring women.

[5]Seamons v. Snow, 84 F.3d 1226, 1230 (10th Cir. 1996)

[6]Oncale v. Sundowner Offshore Servs., Inc., 523 U.S. 75, 78, 118 S. Ct. 998, 1001, 140 L. Ed. 2d 201 (1998)

13

—·—

WHY DOESN'T SHE JUST SAY NO?

Because It's Not That Easy

Courtney was a freshman at university. Her first semester was full of the typical college experiences: awkwardly meeting new friends, attending weekly sorority meetings, and stressing out over finals. By the beginning of the spring semester, she felt she was starting to get the hang of this college thing.

Courtney was cursing herself for taking a 9:00 AM class. Her sorority sisters warned her that early morning biology lessons after late night fraternity parties were not good bedfellows. But Courtney still had that "I can conquer the world" optimism that most first year students do.

So here she was.

Courtney got to class early that day, slid her coat off, and got situated at her desk when a shadow was cast over her notebook. She looked up to see Marcus looming over her. He was a statuesque, six-foot-tall fellow with short brown hair. He wasn't skinny but also wasn't muscular. She didn't recall seeing him in any of the fraternity houses she frequented, so she ruled out any possibility that he was a fellow Greek. No, he was just another poor soul who signed up to learn about molecules at sunrise.

Marcus introduced himself casually enough. Just a hello, his name, and a smile. Courtney had no need for concern. Afterall, it was freshman year; meeting new people was par for the course. She politely said hello back and introduced herself, erroneously thinking that this would be their only conversation.

But it would be far from that. Each morning, Marcus would make a bee line for Courtney's desk for a pre-class conversation. And while Courtney didn't wish to be rude, chatting with Marcus wasn't on the top of her priorities list. Still, if making a few minutes of small talk before class was what it would take to get him off her back, Courtney would begrudgingly participate.

One day in February, Marcus got bold. He suggested that they go hang out sometime and as such, asked for her number. There were several reasons Courtney wasn't interested. She wanted to focus on keeping her grades up. Plus, most of her free time was taken up by her sorority. But quite frankly, she just wasn't interested in Marcus. So, believing that she would only have say it once, she politely declined Marcus' request. But Marcus was persistent. Every time he saw her, he would have a line.

"You know we'd have a good time. Let me call you!"

"Quit playing hard to get."

"Oh, come on Court! Let me get your number!"

After several more no's from Courtney, Marcus changed his strategy. Perhaps asking for Courtney's phone number was too forward. So, he changed his request to her email address instead.

He asked.

And asked.

And asked.

Eventually, to avoid Marcus, Courtney stopped coming to class early. But in the end, she finally acquiesced to his pressure and gave Marcus her email address.

———

It was the end of April and final exam anxiety had set in. Students on campus sequestered themselves in every corner of the library. Sorority house study rooms overflowed. Coffee and energy drinks were bought in abundance.

Courtney only had three exams, two less than last semester. She was anxious but felt confident. After all, she aced them all the previous semester, easily making the Dean's list and her sorority's honor wall.

She was bunkered down in her dorm room, eyeball deep in her U.S. History study guide when her stomach began to growl. She thought to herself that it was probably a good time to take a break as she had studied straight through dinner. She threw on a light jacket and walked out of her dorm building, breathing in the fresh evening air. While there were several places students could get food on campus, there was only one place that carried *her* favorite snack food; a little gas station about a mile away from campus. And for a bag of rich, chocolatey, Muddy Buddy Chex Mix, Courtney would gleefully hop that mile on one foot if necessary. So, with her ear buds planted firmly in her ears, she set off.

———

It only took Courtney about 15 minutes to make it to the gas station. Admittedly, she was a little zoned out; her thoughts split between her music, studies, and snacks. She didn't notice Marcus walk in the store until he was right in front of her.

Courtney had done her best to keep her distance from Marcus since he persisted that she give him her email address. She thought that by giving him what he wanted, he would ease up a bit. But after receiving

20 emails from Marcus in one day, Courtney knew that she wouldn't be rid of him anytime soon. The emails became so bad that she had to delete that particular inbox from her iPhone and quietly set up a new email account. That move was enough to shield her from the digital harassment, but now here Marcus was in person; towering over her with a grin on his face.

Courtney made some small talk to be polite, but did so with a curt demeanor to send the clear message that she was in a rush. Marcus asked which car was hers, to which she responded she had walked. Marcus saw an opportunity. He offered to give her a ride back to campus.

Once again, Courtney tried to be polite in saying no. Marcus may have had good intentions, but under no circumstances did she want to be alone with him. What she wanted more than anything was to be back safely behind the locked door of her dorm room. So, she said no. But just as he did in trying to procure her phone number and her email address, Marcus persisted and tried to guilt Courtney into saying yes. Courtney would say no, multiple times. But Marcus continued to follow her through the gas station, insisting he would be taking her home. When she would try to exit the store, Marcus would use his larger frame to physically block her path.

Courtney was scared. She had adjusted the time she went to class and changed her email address, but now she was being physically blocked in the store with no way around Marcus' demand. So, under extreme pressure and with great reluctance, she submitted and walked to his car.

The ride back to campus was terrible. Marcus made small talk about finals and a couple of parties he had heard about after exams were over. On the exterior, Courtney engaged in conversation, even mustering up a laugh or two. Inside however, she said a silent prayer that she would make it back to her dorm safely. She thought back to all of the times her parents warned her about getting in a stranger's car when she was a child. Now here she was, a grown woman coerced into doing just that.

The ride was only 5 minutes long, but it might as well have been an hour. As Marcus' car pulled up to her dorm, a wave of relief washed over Courtney. She had never been so happy to see the weathered red bricks of her building. Marcus droned on, clearly wanting to sit and chat some more, but Courtney had only one thought in mind. She quickly thanked him for the ride and then bolted out of the car to safety.

Summer had come and gone, and the fall semester was well underway. Courtney had made it through freshman year with stellar grades and her sophomore year was off to a fantastic start. She even had a job at the college bookstore. She hadn't thought much about Marcus since April. She told a few of her sorority sisters about the altercation at the gas station. They agreed that it was creepy and maybe even something she should consider reporting to the school. But Courtney brushed it off in the scuttle of moving back home for the summer. As she no longer checked her old email account, she hadn't seen or heard from Marcus the entire summer break. Then when she came back to campus in September, she breathed easy when she realized she didn't have any classes with Marcus either. Maybe he dropped out or transferred. Courtney didn't care much either way. She was just happy she could go about her classes without any interruptions.

But her peace of mind would soon be interrupted. One day while Courtney was ringing customers up at the bookstore, she looked up to see Marcus standing before her in line. Her heart sunk. Maybe he wouldn't recognize her. Maybe he would be so busy getting his books, he wouldn't have time to talk. Or maybe he had finally gotten the point and would leave without incident. None of these would be her reality. Almost immediately the bombardment of questions began.

"Why did you run off after I gave you that ride?"

"Why haven't you answered any of my emails?"

"Are you avoiding me?"

"What, do you not like me or something?"

The questions came almost too fast for her to answer. Once again, Courtney was scared. She knew being at work would protect her from any physical harm. But his determined persistence brought back the same wave of anxiety she felt sitting next to him in his car all those months ago.

After his first wave of interrogation finished, Marcus then proceeded to request her number. Now this is something Courtney absolutely did not want to give. She could ignore and even change her email address. But her phone number was different. All of her family, friends, and sorority sisters had this number. Her phone was an intimate portal into her life; one she did not want Marcus to have privy to. But it was clear that he had no intention of leaving her line without her number. Other students impatiently waited behind him. Marcus kept talking. Courtney felt light-headed. Before she knew it, she had given in. Maybe he wouldn't use her number. Or if he did, maybe a few unanswered texts would finally drive the message home; uninterested. Once again however, this was wishful thinking.

————

The texting began that evening. Courtney physically cringed when she heard the tone on her phone go off. She already knew the identity of the sender without even looking at the message. The first texts were simple enough.

"Hey Courtney, how's it going?"

"So how was your summer?"

"You sure looked good today at the bookstore."

Courtney didn't respond. Maybe if she ignored the texts then he would get the point. He would leave her alone. He would move on. But he wouldn't.

The next morning Courtney woke up to over 30 messages. He had texted her all through the night, long after she laid her head down. She was shocked. It appeared her strategy of avoidance had the opposite effect.

"I don't know why you keep avoiding me for."

"I just want to talk."

"We should hang out soon."

"You should let me take you to dinner."

Courtney sat in the middle of her bed speechless, looking at the one-sided conversation in front of her. And it didn't end there. Throughout the day, he would message.

During Chemistry:

"How's your morning going?"

During Lunch:

"Hey, I'm about to grab something to eat. Wanna join?"

During Algebra:

"What is your class schedule for this semester?"

By the time Courtney made it to her job that evening, she was on edge. When would the messages stop? Or even worse, would he come back to her job? Every time the store's motion sensor doorbell would ring, Courtney's heartbeat would increase, and her eyes would dart to the front door.

Was it him?

Usually, Courtney would leave her job full of energy, ready to tackle her homework in the school library or watch TV with her dormmates.

But ever since the calls began, her head had been on a swivel, never knowing when Marcus would catch her off guard. Her energy and bright demeanor had faded; replaced with anxiety and nervousness.

Finally, at the advice of some of her older sorority sisters, Courtney sought out the University's Title IX coordinator and filed stalking and sexual harassment claims against Marcus.

Because Rejection Isn't Normalized

The ability to decline the romantic advances of another is a right that women should be able to exercise freely and liberally. While being the recipient of rejection can be soul crushing and humiliating to some, romantic rejection is normal and healthy part of the dating process. Rejection shows us that women (and men) have options in who they chose as their partner. It reflects our personal preferences and defines our standards.

Despite this, simply saying no has its difficulties as romantic rejection has led to male reactions ranging from verbal abuse to stalking to physical violence. In the most extreme cases, it can even include murder. Dr. Suzanne Degges-White, chair of the Counseling and Higher Education Department at Northern Illinois University, has analyzed this issue. She states that:

"Unfortunately, we've spent years trying to build up the self-esteem of an entire generation and have created a world in which the word, "no," carries more power to wound adults more deeply than ever believed possible. The 'everyone gets a trophy' mentality coupled with the instant gratification that technology seems to offer has created a world in which rejection seems like a direct attack on a person's sense of self."

When we look at the social conditioning around the importance of romantic success for men, we began to uncover the roots of this corner of the toxic masculinity profile.

Because Media Teaches Men "The Hunt"

Media such as movies, music, and television have long normalized the overly persistent pursuit of women. Men (typically viewed as the plucky protagonist) will chase their romantic targets despite numerous rejections. Typically, the climax of the story will involve a grand gesture that will finally change the woman's mind, turning her numerous "no's" into the sought after "yes."

Take for example the 1976 film Rocky. In the film, future heavyweight boxing champion Rocky Balboa goes on a date with local pet store worker Adrian. At the end of the date, they wind up at Rocky's apartment where he invites her in. Adrian declines five times, saying she has to go. But Rocky persists and Adrian finally enters the apartment. Once inside, Rocky proceeds to strip down to his tank top and put on some soft music. This all happens within the first 20 seconds of the two walking into the apartment. He then asks her to come sit next to him on his couch. Adrian tries to deflect Rocky's request by making small talk about some old family pictures he has on display, but an undeterred Rocky asks her again to come "relax." The clearly uncomfortable Adrian then asks Rocky if she could use his phone to call her brother because he may be worried. Rocky makes a joke out of this request by hollering for her brother out his fire escape window and then proceeds to advance towards Adrian with his muscles bulging. Adrian says she doesn't think she belongs in Rocky's apartment and expresses that she doesn't know him well enough to be in his apartment (which is a very truthful statement as this was their first date). She very clearly says the words "I don't know you well enough. I don't feel comfortable." She then makes her way to the door to leave, which causes Rocky to dart across the room, putting his hand on the door to prevent her from opening it. He then puts his other hand on the wall, effectively trapping Adrian between the wall and himself. With Adrian pinned against the wall, Rocky takes off her glasses and hat, telling her he always knew she was pretty. He then tells her that he is going to kiss her. Rocky leans in and kisses Adrian on the cheek (Adrian winces when his lips make contact). He then leans in and kisses Adrian on the lips once. The second kiss however, sees Adrian very much into it as the two slowly slide down to the floor and begin making out. All it took was physically trapping a woman against the wall and refusing to let her leave to spark a timeless love story.

Whether or not Rocky and Adrian's kiss scene is sexual assault has been argued on numerous online message boards such as Reddit and MixedMartialArts.com, with the general male consensus being that what happened wasn't sexual assault by 1970's standard. But Rocky's behavior in this scene sends the very direct message that despite saying no numerous times, all Adrian needed was just to loosen up a bit. And the fact that many men in the post #MeToo era still don't see the issue with the scene displays that many tend to agree that all it takes is a little persistence to change a no into a yes.

Another example of the overly persistent pursuit takes place in 1984's Revenge of the Nerds. For the most part, the film is a typical coming of age story. Our protagonists are a group of college students, bullied by the campus jock fraternity for their intellectual prowess. After being denied admittance into Greek Life, the nerds decide to start their own fraternity and search for ways to earn the respect of their peers. Throughout the film, one of the lead protagonists, Lewis, pursues his crush Betty, a cheerleader and member of the popular sorority on campus. Throughout the film, Betty repeatedly turns down Lewis' advances, partly because she's not interested in him and partly because she is dating head jock Stan. Unwilling to take no for an answer, Lewis notices Stan and Betty in an argument during the Greek Week costume carnival and decides to use this as the opening he's been looking for. Lewis steals Stan's Darth Vader mask and follows Betty into the Moon Bounce Room. Once there, he proceeds to have sex with Betty under the guise that he is Stan. Once done, Lewis takes his mask off revealing his true identity. Betty responds by asking if all nerds are as good at sex as he is. Lewis confirms that they are. Director Jeff Kanew and writer Steve Zacharias have both condemned the scene saying that they regret adding it and calling it not excusable.

Yet another famous example in music is Frank Loesser's 1944 hit, Baby it's Cold Outside. The song is structured as a call and response between a female party guest and host. The guest tells the host that she "really can't stay" and that "her mother will start to worry." The host tries his best to convince her to stay the night because "it's cold outside." At one point, the guest questions "what's in the drink" he gave her and states she wishes she could "break the spell." As the guest ponders whether he has slipped her a micky, the host, knowing that he has her now, proceeds to comment on her sparkling eyes and her "hair that looks swell." When she says she should say "no, no, no", he asks if he can move closer. When she finally gives in, he asks what's the point of hurting his pride. We are then left to believe that the host got lucky and all it took was some "charming persistence" (and probably a date rape drug at worst, or an heavily poured drink at less worse).

While some write "Baby it's Cold Outside" off as a harmless tune from a bygone era, there are certainly many modern examples of songs that encourage the hunt. In 2013, Robin Thicke pursued all of the "good girls", repeatedly telling them that he knew they "wanted it" on his summer hit "Blurred Lines," a song that critics say addresses the gray area between consensual sex and sexual assault. Elsewhere in the year, rapper Rick Ross drew controversy with his song "U.O.E.N.O." when he rapped that he "put molly all in her champagne, she ain't even know it." He then "took her home and enjoyed that, she ain't even know it." Molly of course is slang for a powerful form of ecstasy. The song would cost Ross a lucrative sponsorship from the Reebok shoe company.

Be it heavyweight boxing champion, fraternity member, charismatic party host, playboy pop star, or drug czar rapper, the message portrayed is clear; a "no" from a woman can be transformed into a "yes" when the proper amount of persistence is added. Per this form of masculinity, women are conquests for men to eventually conquer. And while the hunt usually works out in the man's favor in cinema and music, the hunt has the potential to lead to much more dire situations in the real world.

Because You Might Get Stalked

Today, Meredith[1] is an attorney who proudly practices in her hometown of Louisville, Kentucky. In 2016 however, she was just starting her legal journey as a first-year student at a law school in the deep south. It was December and with her first semester coming to an end, she decided to put herself back in the dating world, creating a profile on a dating app and swiping away until she met Chad.

Chad checked off all of the boxes that Meredith looked for in a man. Their religious beliefs aligned. His political compass pointed towards "Progressive Liberal" just like hers. And he was also a law student who attended a law school in the upper northeast. Meredith saw Chad as a decent person and despite the distance between them, the two began dating through the end of the year.

The red flags were subtle at first. She thought it was odd that despite once being viciously sick, Chad refused to see a doctor, as he labeled those in the medical field as inferior. And there were also the little things Chad would say to Meredith, like consistently telling her that he wasn't sure that things were going to work between them due to their different nationalities. Then in January, Chad sent her a screenshot of an article about torture tactics. When an understandably upset Meredith asked why would he send her something like that, Chad laughed it off. Although she wouldn't make her move yet, Meredith knew this was when she should have broken the relationship off.

During a phone conversation five days later, Chad once again told Meredith that he didn't think their relationship would work. This time, it was because he didn't think his parents would accept Meredith due to her parents being divorced. This was the final straw. Meredith ended their relationship.

Chad begged her not to end it. In a two-hour phone call, he apologized profusely and pleaded for a second chance. But Meredith held strong. On the call, she let him vent his emotions, but was very clear and firm that she was no longer interested in the relationship.

It was over.

———————

The next day, Meredith sat in her Property Law class. Emersed in theory such as eminent domain and adverse possession, she focused on her professor and furiously typed her notes.

Then her phone rang.

Luckily her phone was on silent, but Meredith was no less horrified to see Chad's number flash across the screen. What could he possibly want after a two hour "please baby, take me back" phone call? Meredith didn't have much time to dwell on it though, as Property Law was her most difficult class of the semester. Chad was undeterred. In the hour and half Meredith was in class, Chad called six more times and once she left class, Meredith was greeted with 60 texts Chad had sent begging for her to reconsider and most alarmingly, telling her he was going to travel to her city so they could "have a conversation."

Despite clearly telling him NOT to come to her town, Chad allegedly made the trip twice, asking her to meet up each time. Meredith wasn't certain he was actually in town, but with her mind harking back to his previous torture tactics text message, she definitely didn't want to find out.

She ignored his messages, blocked him on all social media, and hoped he would stop.

It was the end of January and Andrea was getting ready for her day, when her phone played the tone alerting her of a Facebook message. She opened her inbox to find a message from someone named Adam. Adam said that he was reaching out because he saw her in one of Meredith's pictures on Facebook. Adam had a huge crush on Meredith but was too shy to reach out to her directly. Adam was wondering if Andrea might be able to connect them. Andrea thought this was cute; an old-fashioned school-boy crush! She cheerfully told Adam she would pass the message along.

Meredith was suspicious when Andrea called her later in the day. Why would a complete stranger look through her pictures, reach out to one of her friends in said picture, and profess his affection for her? But as Andrea continue to talk, a chill ran down Meredith's spine with the frighting truth becoming clear.

Adam was Chad.

As Meredith had blocked Chad directly, he started to reach out to her friends and even her family on social media, in an effort to contact her. This was also around the time Meredith started receiving phone calls from numbers she didn't recognize; with Chad on the other line each time. In February, Chad would even contact her using the Facebook page of the law school student organization he was president of. And if the internet and phone harassment wasn't enough, Meredith constantly worried that one night, she may be leaving class and Chad may be waiting for her at her car, of which he knew the model and unique color of.

The stalking was taking its toll. Because Chad knew where Meredith lived, she began sleeping on friends' couches, hoping to avoid an impromptu and unwelcome visit. She began asking classmates for rides to school to avoid the openness of the public bus she would sometimes take to class. She began rethinking her acceptance of a lucrative summer legal job, due to the firm being located in a big city and her fearing for her safety. She even began working out to lose weight, so she could be quick enough to escape Chad if he ever found her.

Meredith sought help from her University's Title IX office. Couldn't they do something seeing as Chad was a student? Unfortunately, due to Chad attending a different school, the answer was no. Meredith reached out to her local police department. A detective took an initial statement and promised to call her back. But that call never came. Meredith would go to the courthouse looking for help. While her classmates were writing their briefs to try out for the school's mock trial team, Meredith was writing a memo to beg for an emergency protective order. But to no avail.

In October 2017, 10 months after they initially started talking, Meredith received a text from a local area code. Deep inside, she knew it was probably a bad idea to answer, but the local area code threw her off. The sender of the message told her he was "seeking forgiveness."

Meredith asked who it was, but the sender would never answer instead saying, "someone, who is sorry."

As Meredith received this text while she was at school and as it came from a local area code (stoking her fear that Chad was in fact in town), she was visibly scared. She knew she would have to leave campus eventually and if he was in town, he could be lurking in the shadows of the parking lot. But Meredith would find help in an unlikely place. Seeing a very distraught Meredith, a small group of ultra conservative classmates approached her. In the past, Meredith would have argued gun control, immigration, and other points of politics with these people. But on this night, it was nothing more than a group of law students, some of them survivors of sexual assault themselves, caring for a fellow classmate.

They made sure Meredith made it home safety and in doing so, concocted a plan to get the evidence Meredith needed to prove her case against Chad. If Chad was in fact in town, they would attempt to lure him into meeting Meredith. But it wouldn't be Meredith waiting on him. Instead, it would be the group, complete with camera phones to document the whole ordeal. The plan would never launch however as Chad perhaps smelling a trap, refused to take the bait and meet her in person.

As the messages begging for forgiveness continued, Meredith finally broke down. "You are getting far too comfortable messaging me Chad," she said. "You're right. My bad" the sender responded, inadvertently admitting that it was in fact Chad behind the messages. Meredith continued by telling Chad that the only way he would ever be forgiven is if he stopped trying to contact her and moved on. It was over. When Chad responded with more banter, it was clear to Meredith that Chad would never take no for an answer.

———

Erin was one of Meredith's new conservative friends she met through school. She was a volunteer for the Trump administration and a year prior, would have been the last person Meredith would have expected to be an ally. But Erin was a survivor of sexual assault. She knew the angst and anxiety that Meredith was feeling because it wasn't too long that Erin had felt it herself.

Erin was also a law clerk for a local district attorney. Over coffee, Meredith shared with Erin her entire story, including her failed pleas to her university, law enforcement, and local judge for help. Erin recommended bringing this up to her boss which Meredith, feeling she had exhausted all other avenues, agreed to. This would start a chain reaction. After Erin told her DA what Meredith had been through, that DA relayed the story to the DA in Meredith's jurisdiction. That attorney would then reach out to the sheriff directly and suddenly, Meredith's file was exhumed from the pile of files it sat under on the original detective's desk.

Meredith received a call from the detective saying "it was handled." The detective had spoken to Chad directly. Chad claimed that he didn't know what he was doing was wrong. He claimed to not know the gravity of his actions. He wasn't trying to hurt or scare anyone. He was just a guy trying to win the affections of a beautiful coed he met online. But the detective was hearing none of it. In an example of men holding men responsible, the detective described Chad's actions as stalking, making sure to highlight the severity of the situation. His message was clear; knock it off or the next time they'd speak, it would be in person, due to a warrant.

And that was it.

No more phone calls. No more text messages. No more contact.

Although she would forever live with some small level of uncertainty, Meredith was finally free.

And all it took was having a contact to a district attorney and a direct threat from a detective, to end her stalking nightmare.

Meredith's story reflects the common statistics reported about stalking in America. Of the approximate 6.6 million people stalked in the United States annually, one out of four are women. The frequency of Chad's actions reflects the statistic of 2/3 of stalkers pursuing their victims at least once per week. Chad also used various means to pursue Meredith, something that is common with 78% of stalkers. Meredith's reaction to Chad's stalking seems to be on par as well, as anxiety, insomnia, social dysfunction, and severe depression is much higher among stalking victims than the general population.[2]

In attempting to understand what leads to stalking behaviors, psychiatrists have developed four stalking profiles. The Resentful Stalker is a self-righteous, self-pitying person who never acts on his threats. The Intimacy-Seeking Stalkers believes he is loved or will be loved by the victim and often focuses on someone of higher social status, such as celebrities. The Incompetent Stalker is socially backward and doesn't understand the social rules of dating and romance, often meaning no harm (if Chad's explanation to the detective is to be taken at face value, he would fit this profile). The Predator Stalker is focused on sexual gratification, control, and violence. The Predator plans their attack, rehearses it, and has lots of sexual fantasies about it. Lastly there is the Rejected Stalker. This person was rejected in a relationship, and perceive it as an insult, feel wounded, and is seeking vindication. The Rejected Stalker is the most common of the profiles and along with the Predator, is also the most dangerous as they are most likely to assault their victims.

The initial motivation of the Rejected Stalker can be one of two things. First, a Rejected Stalker may be trying to reconcile a failed relationship. As seen in Meredith's case, Chad's motivation was attempting to rekindle their short, yet failed, relationship. From harassing her friends to calling her from blocked numbers, the end goal of all of Chad's actions, was to engage Meredith in conversation with the hopes that something he might say, would convince her to give their relationship a second chance.

The second motivation for the Rejected Stalker is revenge for the perceived rejection. They perceive their rejection as a slight and feeling insulted, pursue vindication. Driven by revenge for his ended relationships, in 2018 a Virginia man by the name of Satyasurya Sahas Thumma stalked two former girlfriends. Using a fake phone number, Thumma harassed the first woman by continuing to send her nude pictures and videos he obtained of her when they dated. He would also create a fake Snapchat account, where he would post the photos and videos. He would then share the account with the women's friends and family to embarrass her. In regard to the second woman, Thumma created a fake persona to harass his ex-girlfriend, threaten to share her nude photos, make extortion demands, and threaten violence. Thumma took the manipulation one step further by claiming that the "person" was also stalking *him*. In March 2019, Thumma was hospitalized due to a car accident. While in the hospital, he feigned being passed out and took a selfie of his battered face. Upon leaving the hospital, he texted the picture to his ex from the fake account with the words "you're next." In November 2019, Thumma would be sentenced to six years imprisonment for stalking, amongst other related charges.

Along with the stalker profiles, also comes methods in which perpetrators can be treated and hopefully rehabilitated. For the Rejected Stalker profile, experts state that the therapeutic focus is usually centered on the stalker "falling out of love." The individual is counseled

on how to move on from an angry preoccupation with the past to the
sadness of accepted loss. Dr. Robert Mueller, a professor of psychology from York University, states that in almost all stalkers there is a need
both to improve interpersonal and social skills, and to instill a more
realistic understanding of the impact of their behaviors on victims.

Because Women Who Say No Are Evil

Dr. Dre and Snoop Dogg's seminal 1992 video for their single
"Nuthin' But a G Thang" depicts a day full of fun in Long Beach,
California. The pair (along with Texas based rapper The D.O.C.) pull
up to a cookout in a sparkling clean navy blue, low rider convertible,
complete with gold rims. After a sand volleyball game where a female
player has her bikini top pulled down, the guys cruise around, finally
landing at a house party later in the evening. Everyone is having a
fantastic time, dancing in the living room as the D.O.C. makes a bee
line for a refrigerator filled only with 40-ounce bottles of malt liquor.
Later, a woman dressed in a black tank top and matching black skirt
comes in the party. She wanders through the dancefloor drawing the
gaze of several of the men there. Several reach out and touch her and
one exchanges some words with her which is an exchange she disgust-
ingly brushes off. As she continues her way through the dancefloor,
two men flank her on both sides, equipped with two of the 40s from
the aforementioned refrigerator. The men proceed to shake up the
bottles and spray the women with the alcohol, her punishment for
being "bougie." While the woman is portrayed as stuck up, her only
real sin is rejecting the advance of several men on the dancefloor; an act
that justified the sentence of public humiliation. This scene may have
been played for laughs at the tail end of a music video, but it reiterates
the role cast upon women when they exercise their right of romantic
rejection.

A team of Kansas State University psychologists led by Evelyn Stratmoen, performed a study which saw 60 male and 60 female students complete the Masculine Honor Beliefs Scale (MHBS). The MHBS focuses on how people adopt their masculine beliefs and how they relate to aggressive behavior. As a part of Stratmoen's study, she used the following example:

Tom is at a party. He notices a woman he finds attractive and attempts to catch her eye from across the room. After a few failed attempts to get her to notice him, he walks over and introduces himself. They make small talk and after a while, he asks her if he can have her number. She says no.

The study found that those who endorsed the ideal that masculinity should be honored, were more likely to view Tom as being insulted by the rejection, feeling less of a man. This group would also be more likely to approve of an aggressive response such as grabbing the woman's arm or calling her a slut.

This study helps us understand why women who reject men are labeled as "evil." While they are simply saying "no", often times in a polite manner, some men view their rejection as an insult on their masculinity and thus, and insult on them. And when attacked, retribution is often considered justified.

Stevens Millancastro worked at Mega Western Sales, a business in Palmdale, California. It was there he met his coworker Jane. Stevens took a liking to Jane and in early 2016, eventually asked her out on a date. Jane politely declined, thinking that would be the end of the situation. Stevens had other ideas, however. He became obsessed with Jane, incessantly staring at her while the two worked. Stevens would check her out from head to toe, staring at her while she performed normal office tasks like walking to the printer or to the filing cabinet near her desk. Eventually Jane reported Stevens' behavior to her boss who reprimanded him for his behavior. But that still wouldn't be the end.

In November 2016, Jane began to notice that her water bottles on her desk began "looking cloudy." On January 9, 2017, Jane noticed a third cloudy water bottle on her desk and reported it to her supervisor who then set up a surveillance camera. Both Jane and the supervisor would be shocked at what the footage revealed. Stevens was recorded masturbating and repeatedly smearing his semen on her computer keyboard, mouse, in her honey jar she kept in her desk, in the lotion bottle on her desk, and in various water bottles. While Jane was able to detect the contamination of the water bottles, she didn't know her honey jar had been tampered with, thus consuming Stevens' semen through the honey numerous times.

Stevens' attorney would claim that his client's crimes were committed out of revenge. Orange County Superior Court Judge Kathleen Roberts would call his crime sexual revenge and call it a "sophisticated scheme to get Jane to ingest his semen after she reported him." The judge also noted that Stevens' anger grew out of control and that he couldn't control his anger or himself. Stevens was convicted of two counts of battery and three counts of assault. He'd be sentenced to 2 ½ years imprisonment and a lifetime registration on the sex offender registry.

While Millancastro's case may be extreme, a more common example of retribution against the "evil woman" is the typical catcalling trope. Abby,[3] a communications professional from Louisville, Kentucky, has been on the revenge end of catcalling numerous times and says that it is a common experience for women. She recalls a particular story from 2008 when she was out in the city's Irish pub district one autumn night, having a few drinks with her friends. She looked down at her watch and realized she needed to leave as she was to meet her boyfriend for a late dinner. As she walked down a side street to get to her car, she heard a voice calling to her from the opposite sidewalk.

"Hey sexy! Let me holler at you" the caller yelled.

Abby tried to be polite in waving him off. She hoped that telling him "thanks, but I have a boyfriend" would be a peaceful resolution to this awkward and unwanted interaction. But it wasn't. Almost immediately, the man would cross the street and began following Abby, constantly calling her a bitch. He would tell her that he didn't believe she had a boyfriend because "no one would want someone as ugly, flat-chested as her," a curious critique seeing as mere seconds prior, she was attractive enough for him to hit on. Abby's rejection of him turned her from admired to reviled. Luckily, Abby saw a few friends further up the street. Sensing the energy was off, they called her over to them, which caused her follower to immediately shut up, cross the street, and disappear into the night.

Catcalling leading to verbal vengeance against the "evil woman rejector", isn't just limited to occurrences on the street. During her time as a public defender in Louisville, Stephanie[4] defended a client in a 2017 criminal matter. Two years after the case, she received a letter from her client claiming that he wanted her help in a family court issue. He also made a romantic move stating "he always thought that they had a connection" and that if she could wait until he got out of prison, he would like to make a relationship work. Stephanie wrote him back saying that she could help him with his family court matter, but ignored his romantic requests, making no mention of them in the letter. The second letter that she would receive took a far more vengeful tone, as the client called Stephanie a "cold, heartless, bitch" for ignoring the romantic elements of the letter. He would claim that she had "played with his heart and emotions" all because she was nice to him when she was his attorney. Stephanie agrees with Abby that the vengeful verbal response to rejection is an experience that is common to most women. Stephanie's experiences include being berated by a bar patron for not allowing him to take a body shot off her, having a drink thrown in her face after rejecting a man's advances, and being verbally harassed after refusing to give her phone number to a man who bought her an unsolicited drink. Today, Stephanie consistently carries a firearm with her everywhere she goes. She states that she never carried a firearm out of fear in her neighborhood, but rather out of fear of a man taking something wrong.

While some may view Stephanie constantly being armed as severe, when a man believes that a woman is evil as a result of a romantic rejection and decides to issue punishment, the outcome can be far more dire than getting called a name or being showered in beer.

Because it May Get You Killed

The word J'Ouvert comes from the French jour ouvert which means daybreak. It signals the start of Carnival and in Brooklyn, the colorful West Indian Day Parade brings thousands out annually to celebrate all things Caribbean. In 2016, Tiarah Poyah was one of the many who came to see the floats, taste the cuisine, and dance to the music the parade is known for. She was 22 years old and in her last year at St. John's University, studying to achieve her goal of becoming an accountant at a top firm.

It was 4:00 in the morning when her and several friends were walking along the parade route, reminiscing about their day. She was then approached by 20-year-old, Reginald Moise. Moise came up to Poyah and without consent, began grinding on her. Tiara rightfully told Moise to "get off her." Moise responded by pulling a handgun out and shooting Tiara in her eye, ultimately killing her. This would hardly be the only slaying of a woman for romantic rejection in 2016.

In January 2016, a 29-year-old Pittsburgh woman named Janese
Talton Jackson was enjoying a drink at a local bar when she was approached by a man named Charles McKinney, who asked her if she
knew where he could find marijuana. Jackson simply said no, and
Charles moved along, talking to other bar patrons. At a little after
2:00pm, Jackson left the bar only to be followed by McKinney who
"positioned himself against her backside in a sexual manner" as a witness would later state. Jackson would gently push McKinney away and
tell him to "chill." She would cross the street, but McKinney would
approach again in the same manner. Jackson would reject his advances
once again, however this time McKinney would respond by pulling a
gun and shooting Jackson. A friend would rush to her, cradling her
on the sidewalk as Jackson's life slipped away.

Two years prior in Detroit, Mary Spears, a 27-year-old mother of
three, was at an American Legion post with several relatives. They had
just left a funeral and were celebrating the life of a recently deceased
relative. Somewhere in the evening, Spears was approached by a man
named Mark Dorch. Dorch asked Spears if he could get her name and
number. She would decline stating that he had a boyfriend. But Dorch
was not deterred, continuing to harass Spears throughout the night.
Dorch was thrown out of the bar but proceeded to approach Spears
in the parking lot. He would then punch Spears, inciting a brawl with
the family. Dorch would then pull his gun and shoot Spears once.
When she tried to run from him, he shot her twice more in the head.
He would also shoot five other family members although they would
survive the attack.

In a 2016 article in the Huffington Post, Zeba Blay wrote about
these incidents, tying the murders to black male fragility. Male fragility
however, is hardly an issue limited to the black community. Be it
Wisconsin's Christopher O'Krowley, who in 2016 shot and killed his

coworker Caroline Nosal for rejecting his numerous sexual advances, or California's Elliot Rogers, who executed a "Day of Retribution" that killed 6 women as an act of revenge for numerous romantic rejections in his life, male fragility transcends race. As writer Clementine Ford explained in her 2016 piece "When Entitlement Meets Rejection":

"The thinking that motivates men in India and Pakistan to throw acid on women who 'dishonor' them in some way is the same thinking that sees a man kill a woman in Pittsburgh because she didn't want to have a drink with him. It's the same thinking that empowers a man in Australia to persistently drug his colleague because she didn't reciprocate his romantic desires."

In my essay "Fruit of the Poisonous Tree: How Toxic Masculinity Produces Sexual Assault," I describe at length how entitlement, the thought that men are owed something just because they are men, is one of the building blocks of toxic masculinity in the sexual assault realm. Male fragility then, is the inability to accept that one is not entitled to something. And as Kate Manne, author of the book Entitled: How Male privilege Hurts Women states, "when women deny men what they are wrongly deemed entitled to, she will often face misogynistic threats and punishment."

Elsewhere, other research suggests that men who classify as socially dominant are more likely to engage in violence as a reaction to romantic rejection. Dr. Fiona Barlow from the University of Queensland, describes socially dominant men as ones who support inequality and are usually less supportive of women's rights. Her research includes two online surveys that polled over 550 men and produced results which showed that socially dominant men tend to express hostility towards women including the desire to discipline them. Regarding romantic rejection, Dr. Barlow states that the socially dominant man, "blames women for rejection, rather than accepting that women may sometimes not be sexually interested." Men who subscribe to long-standing beliefs that they should be dominant in their relationships, are also more likely to use violence against women.

The fact that women must fear for their lives while exercising their right of rejection is vexing to say the very least. But as we have seen, when the fragile male ego meets toxic masculine behavior and beliefs, it creates a level of chaos. And it is this chaos that threatens the innocent lives of women globally.

Because Men Must Discuss Romantic Rejection Best Practices

"I believe the day men start having honest conversations about romantic rejection, they will stop killing women."

Siwaphiwe Myataza, 2020.

The heathy handling of romantic rejection should be taught to young boys alongside other "birds and bees" conversations that parents have. Lydia Bowers is a speaker and consultant from Cincinnati, who provides early childhood education, coaching, and consulting on sexual health topics. She states that "the earlier you discuss rejection with kids, the better, as learning how to cope with rejection is key to understanding consent as a whole." She continues to state that "while consent education is getting more attention of late, we're absolutely missing that rejection piece."

Ohio's Dr. Melissa Martin states that "when you dialogue with your child that rejection is a possible outcome, it won't seem as big as a tidal wave." She recommends starting by telling your elementary school kid that not everyone will reciprocate their warm and squishy feelings. And he or she will not reciprocate everyone's "fuzzy feelings" either. And while these conversations can certainly be steered by mom or dad, having an older male family member lead this narrative (for boys), sends the added messages that (1) it's okay for males to be rejected and (2) it's okay for males to discuss rejection with one another. As fathers (and other male relatives) play a significant role in building the masculinity profile of their sons, personal stories of romantic rejection and examples of healthy coping goes a long way in normalizing health responses.

Past adolescence, the conversation of healthy rejection responses must continue with adult men. The group, A Call to Men, is a violence prevention organization that educates men worldwide on healthy, respectful manhood with the thought that embracing and promoting a healthy, respectful manhood prevents violence against women and harassment. The Canadian group, Next Gen Men, seeks to redefine what manhood means, so that men will experience less pain and cause less harm. While groups such as these provide a great service, the question arises if their message is making it to the street or not. A man willingly going to these websites, listening to their podcasts (and even reading this essay) at least has the base knowledge that there is an issue with toxic masculine behavior. But what of the men that do not see an issue? What of the 1.6 million men who respond negatively to an advertisement from the Gillette Razor company which called men to challenge themselves to be better? What of the men lurking in the corners of Reddit that dismiss toxic masculinity as nothing more than a feminist plot against manhood?

Simply put, street level advocates are needed to hold other men responsible in places where academic rhetoric and gender theory do not normally loiter. Perhaps that is a friend helping another talk through a bad break up. Maybe it is a roommate advising another to "let it go" after being rejected by a Bumble date. Or it could be a teammate interjecting themselves in and de-escalating a potentially harmful situation at a party or in a bar. Whatever the case, street level advocates who hold their peers responsible, translate healthy rejection theory into practical practice.

---

[1] The names Meredith and Chad are pseudonyms used at the interviewee's request to protect her privacy.

[2] Eric Blauuw et al., "The Toll of Stalking," Journal of Interpersonal Violence, 17, no. 1 (2002):50-63.

[3] The name Abby is a pseudonym used at the interviewee's request to protect her privacy.

[4] The name Stephanie is a pseudonym used at the interviewee's request to protect her privacy.

14

— · —

(NON-CONSENSUAL) SEX ON THE BEACH: BYSTANDER THEORY

P CB '15

In March 2015, a disturbing video appeared on YouTube. The setting was Panama City Beach, Florida during that year's college spring break. It was the middle of the day and all of the typical spring break props were present; swimsuit clad undergrads, red solo cups, and fraternity flags flying high. In the 40 second clip, it seemed like a normal college trip to the beach. But just out of frame of the camera was what Bay County Sherriff Frank McKeithen described as the "most disgusting, sickening thing" he had ever seen.

Off camera, Delonte Martistee and Ryan Calhoun, two students at Troy University, sexually assaulted an incapacitated and potentially drugged women on a beach chair. George Kennedy, the victim's boyfriend, would later testify that the victim was stumbling, slurring her words, and falling over shortly before the assault. Kennedy would also be a part of the crowd that encouraged Maristee and Calhoun to continue.

While the assault itself is deplorable, equally alarming is what the camera *did* capture. Despite a sexual assault happening on a crowded beach, in broad daylight, no beach goers intervened or called police, instead choosing not to let a gang rape ruin their good time. While troubling, the inactive bystander refusing to intervene with real time sexual assault, is a common issue in rape culture. Sherriff McKeithen ties this incident to inactive bystanders, stating that "within 10 feet from where this is happening there are hundreds of people standing there watching, looking, seeing, hearing what is going on, and yet our culture and our society and our young people have got to the point where obviously this is acceptable somewhere."

I Would Help But...

"It's none of my business."
"Surely someone else will step on."
"I don't want to kill the vibe."

On average there are 433,648 sexual assaults annually in the United States. 30% of those assaults happen with bystanders present. Be it a fellow party goer, a music festival attendee, or a complete stranger walking down the street, many sexual assaults are taking place in front of an audience rather than in the theoretical shadows. Despite these crimes having witnesses that could very well intervene, in many instances bystanders refuse to get involved. Some will watch. Some may even record. But many fail to act. In fact, studies show that the average person only acts 20% of the time when witnessing a problem situation, let alone a sexual assault.

In 2017 Greek Law, a Louisville non-profit organization that educates students on sexual assault prevention, spoke with a group of high school boys about bystander intervention. The boys were asked how they would react if they witnessed a rape. While a majority of the boys stated that they would intervene in some form, a few indicated that they would refrain from getting involved. When questioned, one of the boys stated that while he hoped someone would intervene if his sister was being sexually assaulted, he himself wouldn't intervene in an assault because it would be "none of his business." Not feeling a connection to the situation is just one of the barriers that prevent bystanders from acting.

The Bystander Effect

Homecoming is a night that high school students look forward to all year. Second only to prom, the pageantry of homecoming creates memories that students hold dear for years to come. And for Sarah, she had been eagerly anticipating the pomp and circumstance of homecoming for weeks.

In 2009, Sarah was an outgoing 15-year-old, living in Richmond, California. She was a hard-working student that excelled in her school's honors English class. She spent her free time chatting with her long-distance boyfriend. She had a love of photography, even wanting to join her school's photography club. But her parents didn't like her staying after school due to her commitments at her church, which she attended three times a week.

On the evening of the dance, Sarah entered the Richmond High School gym, in a brand new sparkly purple dress, diamond necklace, and silver shoes. She looked over at one of her friends exclaiming she couldn't wait to get her dance on.

Students present, noticed a lack of security at the dance. Most troubling was a group of 12 to 15 guys, lingering near the gym. Despite not having school IDs, security officers did nothing to break the group up and send them on their way.

Later in the night, Sarah said goodbye to her friends and left the gym to wait outside for her father as he was on his way to pick her up. While waiting, a classmate called her over to the courtyard and once there, Sarah was attacked. Police state she was raped, beaten, robbed, and dehumanized by a group of 10 while the homecoming dance continued on inside the school. Witnesses would later report Sarah being kicked in the head as the boys took turns raping her, even using a foreign object to penetrate her. As the assault happened, as many as 20 people watched the attack. Some even took pictures and shot videos on their cellphones. But no one called the police, attempted to intervene, or call for help from the school staff inside the building. Sarah was eventually taken to the hospital to treat her injuries.

When situations such as this transpire, one of the main questions asked is "why did nobody do anything?" After all, you have numerous bystanders equipped with cellphones watching a sexual crime happen. It may be the presence of those numerous bystanders however, that actually prevent intervention.

Psychologists define the bystander effect as the presence of others discouraging an individual from intervening during an assault or other crime. The theory can be traced back to the 1964 murder of Kitty Genovese. Genovese was returning home from work in the early morning hours when she was approached and eventually stabbed by a man as she was approaching her apartment building. A neighbor yelled out, causing the attacker to run off. He would return 10 minutes later to stab Genovese once again, this time raping and robbing her as well. The New York Times reported that 38 people witnessed the murder, however did nothing to intervene. While the facts of this case have been disputed in recent times, Genovese's murder birthed the bystander effect, a theory psychologists Bibb Latané and John Darley made a career of studying. Latané and Darley highlight two factors that compose the bystander effect.

The Diffusion of Responsibility

Diffusion of responsibility sees individuals failing to act when others are present. The individual assumes that another person will act or has already done so and therefore doesn't get involved.

On a sunny spring day in 2017, screams could be heard at the Hall of Justice in Louisville, Kentucky. A group of around 10 people gathered on the steps of the courthouse and watched in intrigue as a man struggled to shove a young woman in the trunk of his car. The crowd was in a trancelike state, watching the woman yell, swear, and be lifted off her feet by the man. The woman grabbed his cell phone, spiking it on the ground, and sending glass into the air. This snapped at least one of the bystanders out of his daze as he rushed back into the courthouse and alerted the sheriffs stationed by the front door. The potential abductor was swiftly arrested and walked to the jail which was on the next block. The bystanders could be heard talking to each other.

"I thought for sure one of the sheriffs would come out."

"We're right next to the jail, I figured a cop would see it and come."

"I was thinking one of these lawyers might do something."

The statements of the bystanders clearly show that in their minds, the responsibility to stop this situation belonged to the authority figures in the area. After all, this was an assault that was happening in broad daylight in front of the courthouse with the jail on the left and the police station on the right. The assumption that help was on the way meant the bystanders could do just that; stand by.

Studies show that the ambiguity of emergency situations can lead to us shifting responsibility. If it is unclear who is in trouble or what is wrong, others may be slow to act, if at all. In the scene at the courthouse, at first it was unclear whether what was happening was a real abduction attempt or a couple horsing around. It wasn't until the man's cell phone was smashed that it became clear that this was a serious situation.

We may also shift responsibility if we are unsure how to act. Did the courthouse scene require a bystander to physically get involved? Would yelling "hey, stop that", have been sufficient? Or would it be more appropriate for someone to retrieve a police officer or sheriff? Being unsure of the proper method of intervention causes people to not act and shift responsibility to someone they feel more knowledgeable in the given situation.

The Need to Behave in Correct and Socially Acceptable Ways

The second factor Latané and Darley attribute to bystander effect is the need for witnesses to behave in correct and socially acceptable ways. In Sarah's case, "anti-snitching" culture prevented many of the witnesses of her rape from coming forward. Salvador Rodriquez witnessed the assault and was initially arrested; however he would later be cleared of any wrong doing. When asked why he did not alert authorities of the assault as it was happening, Rodriquez stated he was afraid of being labeled a snitch; a labeling that could put his own life in danger. "I live in Richmond", Rodriquez said. "A neighborhood like this, snitching is something you don't do, you know. I mean, I have to walk down the streets in fear or my life", he continues. Salvador would not be alone as at least two other witnesses would give anonymous interviews sharing their fear of being labeled a snitch as the reason they did not call the police during the two-hour assault. As seen here, the overarching social norm of not snitching, guided the witnesses decisions to not intervene.

In the case of the Panama City Beach assault, the nature of spring break itself sets a social norm that was not compatible with intervention. Each year, thousands of undergraduates descend on tropical destinations for a week-long party. Beaches, concerts, and night clubs combine with swimsuit clad students to create a hedonistic environment where alcohol consumption and sexual hook-ups are considered the norm. From 1997-2011, Joe Francis broadcast this idea to an entire generation through his *Girls Gone Wild* video series. A typical video tape would feature an hour's worth of girls on the beach at spring break, flashing their breasts to the camera, usually as an audience cheered them on. Movies such as 2012's *Spring Breakers* have been noted for "pushing the booze and bikini hedonism to the extreme[1]." Print media does its part to convey these themes as well. The website "Reborn Masculinity", which refers to feminism as a threat to humankind, hosts an in-depth guide on "Where to Find Girls In Cancun." Meanwhile, Total Frat Move.com teaches readers "How to Convince a Lady to Let You Pound" on Spring Break. With hedonism and sexual conquest being the promoted norm, it is easy to see why some refuse to interact in sexual assault situations, fearing an interruption of the "anything goes" theme. As Sheriff McKeithen stated, the witnesses were "more concerned about spilling their beer than someone being raped."

The desire for social status also serves as a barrier for intervention. In an October 2018 column in *The Washington Post*, columnist Don Palmerine recalled a sexual assault he witnessed in his youth. Don was invited to a house party where members of the football team would be present. As these were the popular kids in school, Don wanted to become friends with them and perhaps, elevate his own social status. Don recalls being told to go outside and look through the basement window because one of the football players had taken a girl down there. Don and a group of boys peered through the window to see a girl passed out on the sofa. The football player proceeded to pull her pants and underwear off and then penetrate her. The girl woke up and began to struggle at which point, all of the boys ran away from the window laughing. Later in the night, another girl lay passed out in a bedroom. A group of boys (which Don *was* a part of) began playing a perverse game. One boy would turn the lights off and while in the dark, the other boys would grope a part of the girl's body. When the lights came back on, the boys would quickly remove their hands, erupting in laughter. After four rounds of this, the boys would thankfully move on to something else.

Palmerine's story highlights the need for acceptance in social groups that many boys and young men experience during their formative years. As the sense of belonging is the fundamental way humankind organizes itself, many will go to great lengths to achieve acceptance in their club, team, or organization. Many would not dare upset the herd, regardless of its behavior, for fear of being cast out.

Do I *HAVE* to?

In the 1998 series finale of the NBC comedy Seinfeld, the four main characters witness an overweight man being robbed at gunpoint. Instead of helping him, the friends crack jokes about the man's weight while one of them films the robbery. Later, the four friends are arrested and later convicted for violating "The Good Samaritan Law" which requires bystanders to help in such situations. While the two-part episode brought back many old characters and provided laughs one last time, viewers wondered if "The Good Samaritan Law" was actually real.

The answer to the question is yes and no. Good Samaritan laws do exist in the real world, however they are typically used to protect civilians who help those in danger from later legal liability. The purpose of Good Samaritan laws is to encourage people to help others, not require them to. The fictional law in Seinfeld on the other hand, creates a duty to help and brings forth a commonly asked bystander intervention question; are people legally required to help a sexual assault victim.

In the California case *Margaret W. v. Kelley R.*, a 15-year-old girl went to a sleepover where she became intoxicated. Without permission from her parents or the host parent (who wasn't aware the girl had even come to her house), she left the house with a girlfriend and several boys from her school. Upon arriving at one of the boy's house, she realized she should not have been where she was and claimed she felt "stuck." She called her friend that hosted the sleepover, asking if her mother would come and pick her up. The mother, annoyed that there had been boys at the sleepover, declined to pick the girl up. The girl would be brutally sexually assaulted by the boys later in the night.

The girl brought suit against the mother for negligently failing to take action to prevent the attack or protect her. The court stated however, that generally one has no duty to protect others from the conduct of third parties. A person who has not created a peril is ordinarily not liable for failure to take affirmative action to assist or protect another, no matter how great the danger in which the other is placed, or how easily he or she could be rescued.

There is an exception to this if there is some relationship between the parties that gives rise to a duty to act and the danger was foreseeable. Common examples of special relationships include the relationships between schools and their students, innkeepers and their guests, common carriers and their passengers, and hospitals and their patients. In *M.W. v. Panama Buena Vista Union School District*, an 8th grade special education student was sodomized by another student in a bathroom prior to class. The Court found that a special relationship is formed between a school district and its students resulting in the imposition of an affirmative duty on the school district to take all reasonable steps to protect its students. The Court also found it reasonably foreseeable that given the lack of direct supervision in the early morning hours, a special education student such as the minor, was at risk for a sexual or other physical assault. Therefore, the school district was found responsible as it owed the student a duty of care to protect him from the sexual assault.

Given the two elements required in the Special Relationship Doctrine, while Sarah's school may have a level of liability due to a special relationship and foreseeability, the bystanders that witnessed the attack owed her no legal duty of care. The same goes for the Panama City spring breakers and any other bystanders that fall outside of a special relationship with a victim.

Intervening Behavior

Despite the law not requiring bystanders to act, bystander intervention is a much-needed tool in the fight against sexual assault. The Green Dot Bystander Program was founded in 2009 by Dr. Dorothy Edwards, a psychologist and professor at the University of Kentucky. The program uses red dots to represent incidents of sexual assault or misconduct on campus, and green dots to represent proactive and reactive behaviors towards sexual assault. At the heart of her program are the 3D's, which have been widely utilized in groups ranging from colleges to the Marine Corp. The 3D's provide bystanders strategies to intervene in misconduct situations.

Direct Intervention

In March 2007 three former college soccer players, April Grolle, Lauren Chief Elk, and Lauren Bryeans, noticed a young, blond girl at a house party they were attending. They complemented her on her necklace and then went on their way. However, they would encounter her again later in the night. As the three were about to leave, they noticed another female party goer pounding on a set of French doors that had a large black sheet hung to prevent anyone seeing inside. She told April and friends that there was a 17-year-old girl inside with eight guys. When April and her friends attempted to enter the room, they were stopped by a man whose job it was to guard the door. He told the trio that "she wants to be in here and she wants this", before slamming the door. Noticing a portion of the door that was uncovered, the trio peered inside and saw the same blond girl from earlier in the night, passed out on a mattress. With an audience of eight on lookers, one guy had sex with the unconscious teen while another forced his penis in her mouth. Knowing that they were witnessing a gang rape, the trio barged in the room to rescue the girl. "A door couldn't stop us, boys couldn't stop us," Grolle told a local news broadcast. "I mean, it was just fight or flight, and we were gonna get her out of there."

Direct intervention happens when a bystander directly acts to stop a situation from happening. The trio of soccer players from the house party saw a sexual assault happening and used the direct action of bursting in the room to break the situation up. In some cases, direct intervention includes an even more physical action on the bystanders part.

In 2015, Ketrell Fergusion of Washington D.C. had recently found himself homeless. On March 27th, he was searching for a place to sleep when he heard screams and noticed a nearby struggle. Initially, Ketrell thought what he was witnessing was a robbery. However, he quickly realized he was seeing a sexual assault. The attacker, Alemen Gonzalo, had offered a woman money for sex and when she declined, attempted to rape her behind a bus stop. Armed with a stick and remembering relatives of his own that had been raped, Ferguison intervened, striking

Gonzalo numerous times. Police apprehended the subject, who was bleeding from his head, about an hour later.

While the superhero swooping in to physically fend off attackers may sound gallant, physicality is not an option for everyone. In some cases, a physical reaction could put a bystander in just as much danger as the victim. Direct interaction doesn't always have to be physical action, however. In some cases, direct interaction takes the form of a classmate, teammate, friend, coworker, or fraternity member, being the voice of reason in a situation. In 2013, Mack Prioleau lay asleep on the top bunk in his Vanderbilt University dorm room as his roommate and two other members of the school's football team drug an unconscious woman into the room, proclaiming that they were going to "fuck this bitch" while passing around condoms. Prioleau would awaken and later testify that he knew exactly what was going on. But as he was "uncomfortable", he chose to pretend he was still asleep. While Prioleau failed to act, his story outlines a position where nonphysical direct intervention would have been applicable. As Prioleau's roommate was the rapist and ringleader, there already existed a relationship between the two. A quick "come on man, this isn't right" could have very well stopped this rape in its tracks.

Delegate Intervention

"See Something, Say Something" is a mantra that many law enforcement and public safety organizations employ. The idea is simple; if you see suspicious or illegal activity, alert local authorities to it. This form of intervention also applies to sexual assault. In Sarah's case, the opportunities for intervention through delegation was plentiful. First, Sarah's rape happened while a school function was taking place. Mere feet away in the gymnasium, were any number of staff, faculty, and security that a bystander could have alerted to the attack. Second, it was reported that several of the bystanders took pictures and recorded the gang rape on their smartphones; the same phones that could have been used to call the local police. While the fear of being labeled a snitch certainly weighed on the mind of the bystanders in this case, there were several ways for discrete and anonymous intervention.

In some situations, there may be a more suitable third party to delegate intervention to. Prioleau witnessed his roommate and friends, raping a woman in their dorm room. Reporting to a resident assistant, who serves as the authority figure in campus housing, could have perhaps brought an end to the assault quicker than calling campus police. Prioleau would testify that he was "scared and uncomfortable and didn't know what to do." Delegation allows a bystander to involve someone that may be more equipped to handle the situation and is key for those uncomfortable intervening themselves, for whatever the reason.

Distraction Intervention

Intervention through distraction involves diverting and redirecting the involved parties of a potential assault or harassment situation. While Green Dot training recommends asking to borrow a dorm key card from or "accidently" spilling a drink on one of the parties, some bystanders have gotten creative with their distraction tactics.

In a 2014 New York Times article, University of New Hampshire's Daniel Rowe recalled a distraction technique he used on one of his football teammates. Rowe states that his teammate was drunk at a party and kept pressuring a female party goer. Rowe took his teammate aside and told him that while it was clear that the woman he was pressuring didn't want to be with him, there was another woman downstairs that was into him. He led his teammate downstairs, in search of this mystery woman. However, there was no woman downstairs; it was only a ploy for Rowe to lead his teammate away from the situation.

Later in the same article, University of Massachusetts' Lena Ngor shared her strategy for intervention through distraction. Ngor noted that at many of the parties that happen through the semester, she has friends who get intoxicated and need her to rescue them. Ngor recalled being at a party where a guy was "all over" one of her friends. Ngor approached the friend, put her arm around her and told the guy, "She's mine, you can't have her." Intervention through distraction provides great preventative value to situations that haven't yet escalated.

Flattening the Curve

The 3D's may be a common sense based, practical approach to bystander intervention. But does it work? Research [2]from the University of Kentucky shows that bystander education does have a positive effect on those who undertake it. In the research, the largest and longest of its kind, 26 high schools were studied over the course of five years. Half of the schools taught the Green Dot method while the other half offered no bystander intervention training at all. By the third and fourth years of the study, sexual assault victimization rates lowered by 12% at the schools that offered Green Dot to their students There were 120 fewer incidents in the third year of the study and 88 fewer in the fourth year.

In addition to Green Dot, bystander intervention programs like the NASPA Gold Star award winning "Step Up!" Program, makes its mission to educate students to be proactive in helping others. Bringing in the Bystander® highlights the community responsibility approach when teaching bystanders how to safely intervene. And very writer's own high school curriculum, "Just a Few Questions", challenges high school students to identify methods of intervention in a series of interactive fact patterns. Outside of the academia world, the United

States Army utilizes their SHARP (Sexual Harassment/Assault Response and Prevention) program. Founded in 2008, the program's goal is to "eliminate sexual assaults and sexual harassment by creating a climate that respects the dignity of every member of the Army family." With numerous options, bystander intervention is more than available for utilization in a variety of environments, from school to workplace to the armed forces.

Most reasonable people understand that sexual assault is wrong. And as such, they may desire to stop assault when they see it, even if they aren't sure how to do so. Bystander intervention education is a necessary tool as it helps people understand their unique intervention barriers while helping to identify solutions that are within their comfort zone and are appropriate to the many situations they may encounter. If sexual assault is to be looked at as a community problem, then it takes just that to solve it; a community.

[1] Meyer, Carla (March 22, 2013). "Movie review: James Franco only non-vacuous part of Spring Breakers'". The Sacramento Bee. Retrieved November 18, 2013.

[2] RCT Testing Bystander Effectiveness to Reduce Violence - American Journal of Preventive Medicine (ajpmonline.org)

15

---·---

WHEN WE CRY

*W*hen we cry, we're called pussy
    When we lash out, we're called thugs
When we hold it in, we're told to express our emotions
While everyone laughs.

It was Sunday, March 27th, 2022; the evening of the 94th annual Academy Awards. In a few moments, legendary drummer Questlove would be awarded his first Oscar for his work on the documentary, *Summer of Soul*. It would be another Philly native however, that would own the next morning's headlines.

Comedian Chris Rock took the stage to present the award. As comedians do, Rock started with a few light jokes. One joke however, hit a little too heavy. When Rock spotted Jada Pinkett Smith in the crowd, with her freshly shaven head, he made a joke about being excited for a G.I. Jane sequel. Unbeknownst to Rock, Jada suffers from alopecia; a condition that causes one to lose their hair in patches, often leading to one shaving their head.

When the joke was made, everyone laughed. Everyone except Jada, who rightfully looked annoyed. A few moments later Jada's husband, Will Smith, took to the stage and slapped Rock in his face.

In front of the world.

On live television.

Once again, the crowd laughed. What a funny scene by two of the industry's heavyweights. On the unedited Japanese broadcast, those watching from home could hear what the American censors muted. From his seat, Smith yelled at Rock, "keep my wife's name out of your fucking mouth." The audience gasped. Had they just witnessed the nicest black guy in the world, assault someone *and* yell the F word? To hammer the point home, Will repeated his request.

The audience was silent.

The fallout was immediate. Celebrities like Stephen A. Smith would say what Will did was "bullshit and he was lucky he didn't get his ass kicked." Hall of Fame basketball legend Kareem Abdul-Jabbar wrote a piece claiming that Will "advocated violence, diminished women, insulted the entertainment industry and perpetuated stereotypes about the black community." Randoms on the internet called Will Smith, of all people, a thug and called for the Oscar he'd win later in the night for Best Actor, to be revoked. With one slap, we had witnessed the breaking point of a man. And now we, the public that played a role in him reaching that point, were here to criticize it.

————

Two years before the Oscar's, Jada made a shocking revelation. On July 10th, 2020, the actress, who has been married to Will since 1997, revealed on her talk show that she had an extramarital relationship with singer August Alsina. With tears in his eyes, Will sat by and listened to his wife describe the "entanglement" (as she referred to it), which happened during a period of separation between the couple.

The media and public ridicule were immediate. Alsina would release a song featuring rapper Rick Ross called "Entanglement" which featured noteworthy lines such as, "the definition of entanglement is when you get tangled in the sheets" and "you left your man just to fuck with me and break his heart". The word "entanglement" would go viral with its mere utterance returning us back to Will and Jada's personal life each time it was spoken. The image of Will crying on the show was turned into a meme and shared in all corners of the internet in a variety of ways.

For two years, Will Smith was the butt of the world's joke. He was mocked for showing emotion, his wife (and the mother of his children) was called a hoe, and he was ridiculed trying to keep his family together, all on the public stage. For two years Will's trauma cup was being filled until it finally overflowed on March 27th, 2022. Through Will, we can see the barriers men face in sharing their emotions on the journey to mental health.

Real Men Don't Cry

From a young age, boys are taught not to feel. Dr. Audrey Nelson, a contributor from Psychology Today, describes the "thou shall not feel" masculinity commandment many young boys encounter early in life saying:

"This kind of mind-heart disconnect can begin when boys are in the early years of elementary school. You'll see kindergarten and first-grade boys bringing stuffed animals from home to comfort them amid their fear of the social demands of school. They'll even hold hands and put their arms around other boys and girls to show affection and express joy. But by second grade, male indoctrination can begin. Boys can be considered "sissies" if they show fear, pain, or heaven forbid the most taboo expression of all: crying."

Phrases like "boys don't cry", "take it like a man", and "don't be such a girl", serve the purpose of reinforcing this toxic masculinity law whenever a boy expresses any feeling that can be interpreted as weak, like crying or being sad. While they can be commonly heard as a part of playground chatter, they are also heard in the home as well.

In a 2021 story for *Indy 100*, a 16-year-old boy shared his pain and anger he was experiencing as a result of his father. The boy had tried out for his school's soccer team and was obviously crushed when he did not make it. With his time in high school quickly running out, there wouldn't be many more opportunities to play the sport that he loved for his school. When he got home and into the shower that evening, his emotions rose to the top. He states that he began crying because he felt like a disappointment for not making the team in the small period of eligibility he had left. After drying off, he went to his room and began to cry again at which point, his sister came to console him. Not too soon after, his mother joined in comforting him. When his father entered the room however, the chastising began. His father began a lecture about how when he was young, he never cried and encouraged his son to "try and sound like a man." The father would then state his son was stupid for crying over the situation and he needed to man up.

Even this author can recall many incidents where my audacity to be vulnerable was ridiculed. In 2006, I had suffered an extremely painful breakup with my long-term girlfriend. This break-up came at a major transitional part of my life. In college I was the "big man on campus", VIP at every house party there was to attend. But now that time was over. The fact that I was a subpar student with a low GPA and no real postgraduate plan, made letting go of five and a half years of college life to be thrust into the professional world, a very scary and high anxiety transition. Though I can't recall exactly what triggered me on this particular day, I do recall collapsing on my grandmother's bed in loud, ugly tears. When my mother walked in the room, I was met with neither compassion nor empathy. Instead, I was told to "grow up" and be thankful I was starting a brand-new job the following Monday. My mother's response to my anguish wasn't uncommon. Most displays of vulnerability and distress in our house, were met with accusations of "immaturity" and requests to either "grow up" or "get my priorities in order."

"Young boys are given a small box to choose emotions from", says Dr. Michael Day, the Director of Counseling and Psychological Services at Indiana University Southeast. "When society structures anger, aggression, excitement, and happiness as the 'acceptable' emotions for men, boys grow to view emotions like fear and sadness as weak or 'girly'", Day continues.

Henry Lucas from Louisville Health & Healing, also speaks of the box young boys are placed in. "We are put in a box at a very early age by the messages such as 'Suck it up', 'Don't be a sissy', and Don't be a girl", Jones says. "So, we grow in this box that not only contributes to how we conceptualize what it means to be a male but also teaches that to be outside of the box is to be equal to the opposite sex."

As boys are taught a limited range of feelings, it becomes easy to understand how men can mishandle emotions they don't understand. "When you see men act out later in life be it through a violence or some other method, it's all a way of coping with what we don't understand and what we can't explain about ourselves", says Henry.

While men of all races endure these masculinity expectations, the black experience in America adds a unique wrinkle for black men who dare to show emotions that would perceive them as week. In a 2017 article for *Her Campus*, contributor Miranda Perez traced the black need to convey strength back to colonization era. Perez states:

"Black male slaves were sold based upon being the cream of the crop. Most slave owners sought for slaves that appeared to be strong in order to work on the plantations; slave auctioneers thus sold the stronger slaves for the best dollar. According to *Affinity Magazine*: black men who did not fulfill this presumption were raped, beaten or killed. These actions affected how black men were raised to act in a society that was -and still is- against them. Presently, men of color are expected to live up to a standard of machismo. Society expects men to be detached and fearless beings, because that is what makes them "stronger" than their female counterparts."

With this historical foundation, the road to mental health for a black man in America is paved with not only toxic masculinity, but also a strong undercurrent of racism as well.

"He Has Money to Afford a Therapist"

While Smith's outburst gave the world new material to create memes about and became the talk of the social media world for several weeks. Few were willing to have a discussion about mental health. Power 105.1 radio host, Charlamagne the God, shared his take on the situation saying:

"Listen, I love Will Smith and I love Chris Rock and I said this earlier, but I'll say it again, I've gone to enough therapy to know that slap he gave Chris Rock, that joke was a very, very, very small part of the reason. I don't what the 'why' is but for Will to react like that, there is something way deeper going on inside of him that we don't know about."

Still, when faced with a conversation on mental health, many were dismissive. In a Facebook conversation had with a colleague, I argued that Smith seemed to be a man whose cup of trauma had finally been filled to the brim. The colleague responded dismissively by stating that since Will was rich, he can afford good therapy. While certainly therapy is a beneficial tool, masculinity when practiced toxically, can present a barrier to this form of help.

In a 2021 article in *Orlando Health*, Dr. Siddharth K. Shah high-lighted several masculinity barriers men face preventing them from approaching therapy. She states that both traditional gender roles and perception play a role. "Some dislike the idea of being dependent on medications or therapy to be functional or feel happy", says Shah. She continues saying "though most wouldn't hesitate to seek medical care for a broken ankle or take medication for high blood pressure, some men may worry they'll be perceived as weak or broken if they need therapy or medications to help with depression or anxiety."

Dr. Day agrees with Dr. Shah's statement and points to perceptions we have of the mind and body. "The mind has a reputation as some-thing we should be in complete control of and that isn't 'corruptible' like the body", Day says. "So, if the mind has a problem, some men view that as a moral failing. As such, going to therapy is to admit that moral failing."

Shah also points to men's difficulty expressing emotions stating, "men may struggle to verbalize their feelings or share them with others, coupled with the ingrained belief that they should "man up" and deal with it themselves." Participating in therapy requires a level of vulnerability that can serve as a barrier based on how vulnerability has been taught. Day says, "if boys are taught vulnerability as a weakness, then men will avoid anything that makes them vulnerable, such as therapy which can be a help emotion management tool."

Once again, while making it to a therapist is a difficulty for many men, black men have our own unique set of barriers tracing back to the colonization era. In this era, that accepted thinking was that African Americans could not be mentally ill. The common belief was that a man had to own property and actively engage in business and civic affairs to experience mental illness. As African American slaves "had nothing and nothing to worry about," they then, could not be considered mentally ill. When both the 1840 and 1850 U.S. census found such low rates of mental illness among slaves, it was concluded that slavery actually protected slaves from the known diagnoses of the time. Yes; mental health was used to promote and support pro slavery views.

Gatekeeping in the black church serves as a contributing factor as well. "Many still believe that there's no need to go and sit on a stranger's couch when they can find what they need in the safety and comfort of a pew, or in prayer with the pastor", says therapist Logan Wilson, who specializes in black male trauma. As such, there are still strong beliefs in the black church that mental health illnesses, such as depression and anxiety, are the results of the lack of faith or can be "prayed away."

With this as a foundation, it is no surprise that black men's mental health is a complex puzzle. The American Psychological Association attributes structural racism and Black men's unique history in this country as two of the primary reasons black male mental health is intimately tied to factors such as implicit bias on the part of medical providers, high poverty rates, and low access to quality psychological and psychiatric services. As a result, black men harbor feelings of mistrust toward mental health systems such as therapy. Only 26.4 percent of Black (and Hispanic) men ages 18 to 44 who experience mental health challenges actually seek treatment. Regardless of one's social-economic standing, a black man's quest for mental health cannot be oversimplified to "just go to therapy."

When the Cup Runneth Over

"When we suddenly "snap" and become violent, many of us feel that our outburst is wrong. We may find it deeply out of character. We often feel remorse right afterward.

So, what's going on here?"

-Matthew Legge

When Will stormed the stage, drew back his arm, and slapped Chris across the face, I was unbothered. It was a skit. There was even laughter from the studio audience. When he yelled, "keep my wife's name out of your fucking mouth", I was confused. So was the audience. There was an audible gasp. When he yelled it again, this time louder, I knew what I had witnessed. Will Smith snapped.

Flo Conway and Jim Siegelman, authors of "Snapping: America's Epidemic of Sudden Personality Change", discuss some of the contributing factors to a person having a breakdown. They highlight people that are expected to achieve a high level of success in both their work and personal life and those that have high professional demands. They also note those who are required to hide their emotions. When you consider that Will Smith is one of the most all-time successful actors who's public persona is that of the "nice, profanity free, black role model that always turns the other check", it is easy to understand the stress that ultimately led to his pipes bursting.

Virginia Tech Carilion's Chair of Psychiatry and Behavioral Medicine, Dr. Robert Trestman, states that people snap when their ability to cope with stress is overwhelmed. "For some, minor stressors add up, producing a 'hassle factor'", said Trestman. "For others, one overwhelming event can send a person over the edge", he continues. Trestman also points to the way young boys are taught to handle stress and trauma as a contributing factors. "In our world, we have not structured the community supports and skills training for kids to develop adequate, flexible coping strategies," he says. When one's hassle factor has reached its capacity, stress is emitted, often times in combustible ways.

When I was in fifth grade, I tried out for a vocal solo in a Christmas presentation my school was to give. Trying out for this particular solo required me to sing in front of my entire class. The tryout was not good. I did not get the solo. What I *did* get however, was a days' worth of antagonizing from my classmate Jared. I couldn't do a single thing for the rest of the day without Jared laughing, pointing, and leading the rest of the class in coordinated taunting of me. I went home that day feeling pretty low. Of course, I didn't dare take my feelings to my mom as I knew her response would be to (1) simply ignore him (which any bullied elementary school kid can tell you is an absolute impossibility), (2) get my priorities in order (which was math and science, *not* singing), and that (3) I needed to grow up (just for good measure). So, I sat on that trauma and dreaded having to go back to school the next day.

The next morning, I arrived in the classroom hoping Jared had forgotten about my blunder the day before. No such luck would come. My butt wouldn't even touch the seat before the teasing started. By the time lunch was over, I was at my wits end. We were standing in line about to turn a paper in when I could her his mocking voice in my ear. Without a word, I turned and shoved him. The shove caught him off guard and he stumbled backwards, falling over a desk. I then jumped over the desk, raining down blows through a fury of yells and tears (mine). I had snapped. While this incident earned me a three-day suspension, sometimes the result of unmitigated stress can be far greater.

In April of 2014, 7-year-old Kalyb Wiley Primm had endured a day's worth of teasing and bullying. Kaylb, who is a black child with a hearing impairment in one ear, was "antagonized to the point of frustration". This bullying led him to stand up and start crying and yelling. A member of the staff ordered the school resource officer to deal with an "out of control" student. The incident led to Kaylb being handcuffed for 15 minutes until his father arrived. The traumatization of the experience necessitated Kaylb to be homeschooled for the next two years before he could return to public schools.

While Kalyb, Will, and my cases are examples of unchecked emotions leading to the public meltdown or snapping, men's avoidance of feelings also lead to a greater risk of suicide. In 2018 men died by suicide 3.56 more often than women. Dr. Jerry Kennard, a psychologist and associate fellow of the British Psychological Society, attribute being bullied, relationship breakdowns, social isolation, and mental illness as a few of the common risks of male suicide. He further explains stating:

"Men are told they need to be tough and that they should not need to ask for help. Such rigid gender norms may make it difficult for men to reach out and ask for support when they need it. We often do not disclose feelings of depression to their doctors. When we do, it is often described in terms of having problems at work or in relationships. Men also tend to describe their feelings as 'stress' rather than sadness or hopelessness."

Suicide is an even larger issue for black men. A 2022 report from the *Journal of the American Medical Association* showed that black male suicide rates had risen faster than any other racial group, increasing nearly 80%.

From violence to emotional outbursts, to taking one's own life, when one's trauma cup overflows, the spillage can be tragic.

Breaking the Toxic Stigma

Anytime one seeks to change a longstanding culture, intentional actions are required to facilitate the change. If the goal is to encourage men to confront emotional stress and trauma in a more open and healthy way, the first step is to create an environment that combats the mistrust and social stigmas we know exist. This comes when we intentionally avoid trivializing depression in men. Doing so requires adopting an approach grounded in compassion rather than judgement when responding to boys and men. Simply put, we must realize when someone is having a human moment.

Think back to Kaylb's story and his teacher's judgmental response to his display of emotion. The teacher wrote Kaylb's crying off as "bad behavior", leading to him being handcuffed by the school's security officer (an act that wound up causing even more trauma in Kaylb's life and sent the message that displaying emotion, leads to punishment). Compare Kaylb's teacher's response to that of a teacher discussed in a 2017 story from *Hand in Hand Parenting*. In the story, a class of toddler aged students were preparing to go outside for recess. One child, Tommy, wanted to stay inside and play with his friend Zack. When Zack declined and went outside to play, Tommy exploded into tears. Instead of the harsh response Kaylb's teacher applied, Tommy's teacher stayed with him, listened to his crying, and asked a few questions to understand the root of his emotion. The teacher would patently listen and console Tommy until he finally left her side and joined his class on the playground. This teacher's empathic approach not only calmed the situation, but more importantly sent the message that it is okay to cry, vulnerability is natural, and that it is okay to accept help.

Another important approach to reshaping masculinity is for men to openly model compassionate behavior. Young boys must be able to see the male role models in their lives express and show emotion for them to understand it is okay for them to do so as well. Simple acts of warmth like hugging a son and saying "I love you" shows boys that it is okay to express their own affection for others. Likewise, being open with your emotions, (perhaps shedding tears of sorrow at a funeral or those of joy at a wedding), displays that it is in fact, okay for "real men to cry." The use relatable pop culture situations also serve as great platforms for teachable moments. Will Smith's case is a perfect study of the emotion of anger and the consequences that come when improperly exhibited; in Will's case, a decade's long ban from the Academy. A case such as this can be used to teach other healthy alternatives to handle anger inducing situations.

Opening the lines of communication is another step to destroying toxic masculinity mental health stigmas. The fact is that when someone is suffering from depression, sharing their feelings and emotions is necessary to help them cope with the problem. Sometimes this step can be as simple as sending a text to a friend you know who is going through something traumatic. "Checking on your folk" (as it's known where I'm from) is a small act that can address the isolation and helplessness that some feel in a given situation. "There is nothing wrong with having the fellas over to play cards and using that as a distraction to segue that into having some conversation," Henry says. Even communication as simple as a text message can open the door for healing. "It can be a simple 'hey, how are you?' or a 'I know you are going through this thing, I just wanted to say I'm thinking of you,'" Henry continues. "Part of my responsibilities as a man is 'I got to check on my guys.'"

When I was going through my divorce from late 2016- early 2018, a phone call or text from any of my male friends would have been worth more than gold. Years later when a friend was going through a similar situation, I was very intentional in sending those "hey man, what's up?" text messages. The result was opening a door of comfort where he could share his thoughts and his feelings without fear of ridicule or embarrassment. Understand that each man's willingness to share will be different. Sometimes it may take more than just one phone call to break a multigenerational habit. But the fact does remain that we need to be better friends, better partners, and be the support that our fellow men need.

———

Will Smith will be okay. He won't serve any jail time. His millions of dollars are secure. No one (apart from Chris Rock's pride) was hurt. And he certainly hasn't starred in his last movie. America is a country where something is a big deal until the next big deal. Will Smith will walk away from this and possibly turn this moment into something positive.

But what of the millions of other boys and men that are struggling with stress and anxiety the world over? The millions who also struggle to properly address their emotions? The millions whose emotional mismanagement *will* land them in jail, deplete their funds on court cases, and whose actions will see others seriously hurt or worse?

Will Smith slapping Chris Rock doesn't have to be the "black eye on the black community" that Kareem Abdul-Jabbar claims it is. Rather, Will Smith and Chris Rock can be the two stones that strike each other to ignite a long-needed shift towards healthy masculine practices in emotional management.

We just have to man up.

16

—·—

THE MONSTER AT MY LAW SCHOOL

S eptember 21, 2016

It was 11:24 AM.

I was checking my morning Facebook notifications, while sitting at
my dead-end job when he messaged me. I didn't know much about
him. We went to same law school where he was one year ahead of me.
But we never had class together, or even spoke to one another. Why
was this stranger reaching out to me?

He apologized for his intrusion, then explained excitedly that we
were from the same high school. How did this stranger know this? Was
my hometown public on my page? He asked if I planned to take our
home state's bar exam once I graduated. I told him I did, as I wished to
eventually move back home so my young daughter could have access
to a better school system.

He then suggested that we take a selfie together.

This struck me as an odd request considering we literally just met
each other. I nervously laughed his request off saying maybe we could

snap a shot the next time we saw each other in school, secretly hoping we wouldn't.

We continued our small talk. He told me to keep it to myself, but that he could "hook me up with airline tickets" to anywhere I liked if I would give him 30 days' notice. He said he only did this for people he found trustworthy, another peculiar statement as this was still only our first conversation.

We continued our small talk.

He asked if I was on campus and told him I was. He wanted the selfie. He claimed our high school wanted to write a story about two of its own in law school. Once again, a peculiar statement as two old alumni enrolled in law school is hardly an appealing story for the old high school news rag. Still, I agreed to his impromptu photo shoot. Anything for the alma mater, right?

He said he was on his way.

I stood on my office's steps, awaiting him. After about 10 minutes, I saw his car pull into campus from the main road; plodding toward my building, and eventually creeping to a stop. It was an all-black luxury sedan with shadow tinted windows, hiding the figure within.

He had clearly arrived. Darkness in the daytime awaited me through the sedan's unlocked door.

I entered the front passenger side, the cold air from the vents running a chill over my arms. While the tone of our Facebook conversation had been jovial, the tone of our in-person conversation lacked any of the emotion my mind had attributed to his words. He extended his arm, took the selfie, and that was that. I got out and headed back to my office, shaking the eeriness of the whole exchange off as a product of my stressed, 2L nerves.

A few years later during "the incident", I'd curiously comb through his Instagram feed looking for any clues he may have hidden in plain view about his current situation. After numerous rows of selfies, I would finally see our picture from that day. Due to how we were angled, I couldn't see his face when we originally snapped the picture. But here he sat, all these years later; lips slightly pursed, eyes void of emotion, void of warmth. Two cold eyes, starring back at me, casting a familiar chill over my arms.

September 30, 2016 – May 13, 2017

Nine days later, Facebook would alert me of yet another message. It was him. He sent no words, only two pictures of me, sitting at the bench in a courtroom, during one of my internships. From the distortion of the picture, I could tell it was snapped from the back of the room, using his phone's zoom lens.

No words.

No context.

Just two pictures taken by someone I did not even know was in the room.

That would be the last contact I would ever have with him. I would dismiss our encounters as bizarre and would do my best to avoid him in between classes. But try as you might for avoidance, rumors have their way of rustling through law school halls. Allegations about him and other classmates lurked in the dark corners of the school, murmured to those who were curious.

One classmate's accusations told of a night when she had been at a party, drinking alongside her fellow classmates. As the night approached its end, she claimed he approached her, offering what she thought was a chivalrous ride back to her home. She got into the black car and felt a sense of unease when he drove in a direction she wasn't familiar with.

Was this a shortcut?

An alternative route?

The unease quickly turned to panic as she claimed she realized he was driving her across a bridge, across state lines, to his house.

Her and him, in the all-black car, with the shadow tinted windows hiding the contents inside. Plunging deeper into the night's darkness.

The next day, she claimed he sent her a message encouraging her not to repeat the horror that occurred once they arrived at his home. She claimed he would ominously advise her to "think of her children."

More accusations against him came out. Students would whisper and professors would balk. However, without an opposing testimony at his eventual student conduct hearing, he walked away from all the complaints. In May of the following year, he would don his purple velvet graduation hood, walk across the commencement stage, and seemingly out of our lives.

January 17, 2020

I crossed the street and trudged up the stairs of the courthouse with a stack of judicial pleadings to be filed tucked under my arm, protected against the icy January winds. Another day meant another menial task at the law clerk job I had outgrown many months prior. I passed through the metal detector and paused a moment to warm myself a bit, when I felt my phone vibrate in my back pocket. Was it an employer looking to save me from the professional pit I found myself stuck at the bottom of? I looked at the caller ID to see the name of a classmate I hadn't heard from since graduation.

"He's in the news!"

More texts from other classmates would come.

"They arrested him."
"Oh my gosh, did you hear what he did?"
"He's in jail."

I rushed through my task, then back down the escalator, across the street, into my building, and to my desk. The other law clerks stared at me as I feverishly logged into my computer and Googled his name. And there he was, on a local news channel. The mug shot of his face stared back at me with the same cold, emotionless eyes from our selfie, three and a half years prior. Above his image was the headline in bold font, declaring the reason for his arrest.

"Extraordinarily disturbing child porn case."

Defined

Federal law defines child pornography as any visual depiction of sexual explicit conduct involving a minor less than 18 years old.[1] Sometimes referred to as child sexual abuse images or child exploitation images, federal law considers the production, distribution, importation, reception, or possession of any image of child pornography as a serious crime, worthy of severe statutory penalties.

From the mid-1800s to the 1990's, child pornography was not widely available. Such material existed primarily in the personal collections of private individuals. On occasion, someone would be caught at the border with a VHS tape they purchased abroad. Material would occasionally be secretly traded[2] but only amongst a small, dedicated network. In 1970, the first commercial child pornography magazine, *Bambino Sex*, was published, selling over 10,000 copies in its first week. However, research has turned up barely any information about this publication; perhaps a testament to just how elusive child pornography, even when produced for commercial consumption, was during this time.

As difficult as child pornography was to find in the 1970s, new laws would push the material even deeper into the shadows. Congress passed its first piece of legislation against child pornography with the Protection of Children Act of 1977. The legislation allowed for a maximum fine of $10,000 and up to 10 years of imprisonment for anyone convicted of filming or photographing sex acts involving children. Lawmakers at the time stated that the prosecution of child pornography crimes should not only focus on large-scale distributors, but should encompass individual traffickers as well. The legislation passed unanimously, with several related bills enacted later to strengthen Congress' ban. In 1988, the Child Protection and Obscenity Enforcement Act was passed to criminalize the transmission, distribution, or reception of child pornography via computer. Then in 1990, the Child Protection Restoration and Penalties Enhancement Act expanded the criminal prohibitions to the knowing possession of child pornography.

Despite these laws, the production and possession of child pornography has consistently been on the rise. While the public once thought of the stereotypical child pornography user as a shifty-eyed, trench-coat-wearer, hiding in the shadows, the public arrests of many individuals with good jobs, high community standing, and even celebrity status has shown that even the highest-regarded members of society engage in this crime.

Take for example, Air Force Colonel Mark Visconi. Colonel Visconi, a two-time Bronze Star medal recipient, who was sentenced in 2020 to five years imprisonment for downloading numerous images of child pornography as well as using his camera phone to take pictures of young girls under their skirts. Or, take former priest Christopher Rossman who, in 2019, was sentenced to three years in prison after his archdiocese reported Rossman had downloaded child pornography to his smartphone. Jeffery Epstein was a successful financer who mingled with American presidents and British royalty. While Epstein's status as a billionaire may have been questionable, his crimes would become part of the public record. In 2008 Epstein pled guilty to state charges of procuring a person under 18 for prostitution and felony solicitation of prostitution. In 2019 while Epstein was being charged with several sex trafficking crimes, investigators uncovered a "vast trove" of nude photos contained in a safe inside of his 77 million dollar home. Amongst the photos were those of underage children.

Perhaps one of the most famous arrests was that of former Subway spokesman, Jared Fogel. Fogel became a household name and inspiration to many for his weight-loss journey that saw him switching his eating habits to include Subway sandwiches and ultimately losing over 200 pounds. In 2015 however, Fogel would go from famous to infamous as he was sentenced to 15 years and eight months imprisonment for receiving child pornography as well as traveling to engage in sexual assault with a minor.

The crime of child pornography has grown from its shadowy, niche origins into a multi-billion dollar global industry. Whereas child sexual abuse material was once limited to small subculture, today thousands of websites offer the material all throughout the world. To examine the avenues of distribution for child pornography, we must look to the technological advancements of the modern age.

January 28th, 2020

The rumor mill buzzed for days. His name had laid dormant for so many years. He had been relegated to the fodder of "let me tell you how messed up MY law school was" stories. He was something that would come up after a few beers or bourbons at the campus bar; his stories told in the same tone a camp counselor might adopt to recall a ghost story by the fire. He was something we would all prefer to lock away in a dank chamber, deep in our memories.

But now, here he was.

Resurrected.

Once again relevant.

More details of his latest accusations were made public. The police had searched his house. In it, they uncovered numerous thumb drives containing meticulously organized folders, arranged by month and year. Organized with the same precision that we law clerks used when organizing our legal files. Inside these folders were over a thousand images of children being coerced into doing incorrigible things.

Incorrigible things with other children.

Incorrigible things with themselves.

Incorrigible things with adults.

Incorrigible things with animals. Some of the children were old as 17. Some, as young as one year old.

I laid eyes on him as the evening news reported on his appearance in court. He was led in by a bailiff. Instead of wearing a navy or charcoal suit like the rest of us wore to our judicial jobs, he donned a standard issue, baggy, orange jumpsuit. He strolled to the court table with a sense of gusto, head held high. His body moved with a sense of cocky fluidity that is typically reserved for hotshot defense attorneys (or the clients of hotshot defense attorneys). Just before settling at the table, he turned his head, noticing the news camera pointed squarely at him. For the briefest of moments, his icy eyes seemed to lock with mine. The corner of his mouth twitched ever so slightly into a knowing smirk.

The How

As the internet has expanded, so has the different outlets where child pornography can be found. In 1998, there were over 3,000 reports of child sexual abuse images online, however a decade later those reports increased to over 100,000. In 2014, the number of sexual assault reports would exceed one million for the very first time and in 2018, tech companies would report over 45 million online photos and videos of child sexual abuse; a figure that was more than double what was reported the previous year. In today's digitally driven age, child pornography can be found on a variety of online channels including social networking websites, file and photo sharing sites, gaming devices, mobile apps, and internet forums. Due to its anonymous and secretive nature, the dark web remains a popular source for this material.

The best way to describe the dark web is through the iceberg metaphor. The surface web is the top of the iceberg, visible to us as it protrudes from the sea. It is the ten percent of the internet as we know it. This part of the internet is comprised of websites that can be searched by search engines including social media, news, sports, and retail, amongst many others. The portion of the iceberg that sits directly under the sea is called the deep web. The deep web contains data that simply is not indexed by search engines such as Google and

Bing. Academic information, legal documents, government resources, and scientific reports are examples of type of data commonly found in the deep web. At the bottom of the iceberg rests the dark web. Here, one will find illegal information such as stolen social security numbers and other ill-gotten personal information, private communications, political protests, and many heavily encrypted sites.

In the mid-1990s, the US Navy developed technology to securely communicate intelligence information. The Naval Research Lab developed a system called "onion routing" which allowed users to protect their internet traffic with several layers of privacy. In 2003, The Onion Routing project (TOR) became available for public use. Essentially, TOR is an internet connected network, complete with its own internet browser. When a user connects to the internet through TOR, the user's internet activity is stripped of its identifying information and then sent through a series of relay nodes that encrypt and privatize data. TOR basically makes your internet activities into an onion, surrounding it with layer after layer of privacy and protection; essential for the illegal act of viewing and trading child abuse images and videos.

One could assume that it is a combination of the dark web's elusive and criminal nature, combined with the privacy protections granted by TOR, that makes the dark web such a breeding ground for child abuse images. A look at the FBI's investigations of specific TOR-hosted websites, show just how widespread child pornography is on the dark web. An FBI investigation of a single TOR hosted site revealed the registration of approximately 200,000 members as well as 100,000 non-registered visits in a 12-day period. Another FBI investigation of one of the more notorious TOR sites, found that it contained approximately 1.3 million child sexual abuse images. As stated by a

2016 Department of Justice report to congress, "the expansion of the internet has led to an explosion in the market for child pornography." And the market is booming.

In October 2019, it was reported that hundreds of people were arrested worldwide as a result of an investigation of what has been deemed, "the largest dark web child abuse marketplace." Run by a South Korean man named Jong Woo Son, the site "Welcome to Video" contained almost eight terabytes of data showing sexual acts with children, toddlers, and infants. The site used the bitcoin cryptocurrency for members to pay site fees, granting users their own bitcoin wallet address when they signed up for the site. It would be bitcoin however, that led investigators to Son. Law enforcement agents sent small amounts of bitcoin to the site's payment wallet. As bitcoin transactions are visible, investigators were able to see the payments being moved from the payment wallet to a second wallet registered to Son, using his personal phone number and email address. Son was charged with nine charges in the U.S. in relation to money laundering as well as the producing, advertising, and distribution of child abuse imagery. In addition to Son, 337 users of the site were also arrested and charged. These users represent 23 states and a wide range of countries including Britain, Germany, Saudi Arabia, Canada, Spain, and Brazil.

While outlets like the dark web are known hubs for child pornography, illegal images and videos of minors have also found their way onto mainstream mediums as well such as Tumblr and Kik. Founded in 2007, Tumblr is a microblogging website that boosts over 500 million blogs with users making approximately 13.3 million posts daily. In November 2018, Tumblr was removed from the Apple IOS App Store, citing the presence of child sexual abuse material as the cause. As a result, on December 17, 2018, Tumblr permanently banned adult content on the platform including photos, videos and GIFs of human genitals, female presenting nipples, and any media involving sex acts, including illustrations, Despite the ban, however, child pornography still finds its way on the platform.

(*Authors Note*: Around 2022, Tumblr began to quietly allow nudity back on the platform, issuing a "community tag" that would warn users about posts with adult content. They still claim to not allow hardcore sexual content on the platform, however it's still there if you look for it.)

In September 2019, Pennsylvania state senator Michael Folmer, was arrested for uploading child pornography to the site after Tumblr reported the photo upload to local authorities. Folmer admitted to receiving child porn through the site and in February 2020, pled guilty to possession of child pornography charges for which he was sentenced to serve up to two years in prison. In 2020, a similar incident transpired when a Louisiana man, Lynn Johnson, was caught using Tumblr to view, search, and save child pornography on the platform. As with Folmer, Tumblr reported several images of child pornography being uploaded to the site from Johnson's account to authorities. This led to Johnson pleading guilty to one count of possession of child pornography involving a prepubescent minor, a crime that could carry a sentence of 20 years imprisonment if convicted. While Tumblr's adult content ban may not be the child pornography deterrent they had hoped for, the platform seems to do well when it comes to reporting users that distribute images and videos.

The application Kik was founded in 2009 by a group of University of Waterloo students. The free application is an instant messaging mobile app that allows users to anonymously connect to one another. Like the dark web, it is the application's anonymous nature that makes it a commonly used tool for users to share child exploitation material. In a May 2017 *48 Hours* report, a convicted child molester would describe Kik as a "predator's paradise." Given some of the crimes facilitated through the app, this would seem to be an accurate representation.

While there are many of stories of users utilizing Kik to trade child exploitation material, Thomas Paul Keeler II is an adequate example of Kik's many users. In February 2016, an undercover Homeland Security agent posing as a father with a 13-year-old daughter, made contact with Keeler. The agent arranged a meeting at a Red Roof Inn in Cary, North Carolina where Keeler was to have sex with the imaginary 13-year-old. Keller was arrested on March 24, 2016 as he pulled into the hotel's parking lot. After Keeler's arrest, authorities would uncover that Keeler was a regular user of Kik and a member of over 200 Kik groups dedicated to trading child pornography material. Keeler also served as the administrator of a group that required users to share a child abuse image to be permitted to join to group. Forensic investigations of Keller's phone and computer uncovered 1,433 images and 470 videos of child pornography. In October 2017, Keeler would be sentenced to 240 months in prison. As noted above, Keeler's story is just one of many related to Kik.

Video games have become another area where child pornography is distributed. The video games of today have evolved significantly from those in the 1980's. Whereas classic video game consoles like the Atari and Nintendo allowed users to play their favorite titles in their homes, 1993 saw developers looking towards the internet as the future of a multiplayer gaming experience. In 2007, smartphones began to be popularized and along with them came the popularity of mobile gaming – games played primarily on mobile phones, tablets and other mobile devices. With the built-in access to the internet that most mobile devices have, mobile games allow for players to easily connect through multiplayer functions. Unfortunately, as we have already learned, anytime internet functions are available, there exists the potential for the utilization of this technology for child pornography distribution. In 2019, Emilio Morales from Fresno, California, met an 11-year-old boy while playing the game *Clash of Clans*. Using the game to legitimize a 29-year-old man having a conversation with an adolescent, Morales would suggest that he and the child move their conversation to the Kik app for more privacy. There, he coerced the child to produce and send him sexual images and videos. In May 2019, Morales was sentenced to 14 years of imprisonment for using the internet to coerce and entice a minor into producing child pornography. Meanwhile in Broward, Florida, Anthony Thomas would use the popular game *Fortnite*, to victimize at least 20 minors including a 17-year-old female whom Thomas had sex with. Thomas was arrested in January 2019 and charged with 22 counts of child pornography and other charges for unlawful sex with a minor.

Be it the privacy-cloaked outer limits of the web or commonly played video games, the internet continues to be the main distribution hub for child sexual abuse images. And as more applications and programs develop, more avenues are opened. In 2020, as the world turned to the Zoom videoconference application as a business tool in the COVID 19 pandemic, Michael Oghia from Global Forum for Media Developments reported that a conference he was a participant of, was hijacked. The hacker proceeded to play a sexual video involving an infant. As technology continues to expand, so will the avenues of child pornography distribution.

March 26th, 2020

He did not like being caged. But who would? Who would enjoy being contained in a six by eight-foot cell when, three months prior you had the entire world to roam? Who would enjoy three substandard meals in a mess hall when, three months prior, you dined on fine cuisine at trendy restaurants and cafés? Who would enjoy living in a cold dark cell when, three months prior, you were in the tropics?

He wanted out.

The world was in the beginning stages of a pandemic. Earlier in the month, I washed my hands in a Philadelphia bathroom, listening to my fellow concert goers joke that "this damn Corona really has people shook!" Weeks later, businesses were closed, restaurants were relegated to take-out orders only, and entire cities resembled the ghost towns of old spaghetti westerns. For the country, it was an emergency. For him, it was a chance.

He begged the court to let him out of his cage. He said that incarceration during the pandemic placed a grave risk on his health. He promised he would stay put at his mother's house if set free. The judge could even track him via GPS bracelet to make sure. He promised to come back to face justice for his evil deeds.

He was denied.

Later that evening, my mom would send me a news article from our hometown paper about "that boy I went to school with." He had been accused of threatening a witness. The witness that first reported her discovery of his horrible deeds.

His ex-girlfriend.

She was the one who used his iPad on that frigid December night in 2019, stumbling upon several hidden folders. She opened one of those folders and was mortified to be greeted with over 600 images.

Images of children she believed to be as young as two years old.

Images of children she knew to be his relatives.

He wanted out. She would not speak to him, so he called her mother. 250 times. He was desperate. He knew his fate laid in her hands. He pressured with the threat of blackmail of "ugly things about her" coming forth in trial. He intimidated with threats of involving her co-workers. He pleaded with offers of marriage and spousal privilege. She was scared. But she would not break. He would get in more trouble. And he would stay put.

In his cage.

The Why

While the internet allows for child pornography to be easily distributed and places like the dark web provide a level of privacy, there is no shortage of arrests and prosecution of producers and users of these images. As technology and avenues for the distribution of child pornography grows, so does the sophistication of the tools used to track and arrest users. The Child Rescue Coalition's Child Protection System Program, scans file sharing networks and chatrooms and finds computers that are downloading media depicting child sexual abuse. The program has led to the arrest of over 12,000 child pornography users. Similarly, the U.S. Immigration and Customs Enforcement Department touts their Operation Predator program; an international program that identifies, investigates and ultimately, arrests individuals that possess, trade, and produce child pornography. A 2009 investigation by ICE uncovered a dark web forum called Dreamboard, where members posted and traded countless images of child sexual abuse. The investigation lifted the veil of privacy and identified over 600 members of the forum, leading to more than 70 indictments globally. In total, Operation Predator has arrested over 8,000 child predators for a wide range of child sex exploitation crimes. However, despite the legal risks of possessing child pornography, many remain undeterred. It is important to understand why people continue to risk it all by continuously committing this crime.

One group of child pornography users fall into the category of those with compulsive sexual behavior. The Mayo Clinic defines compulsive sexual behavior as an excessive preoccupation with sexual fantasies, urges, or behaviors that are difficult to control. These urges cause distress and have a negative effect on one's health and/or job. These behaviors may also have serious consequences, such as the potential for legal problems. One of the activities commonly associated to this behavior is the persistent use of pornography.

The combination of compulsive sexual behavior and the persistent viewing of pornography is where some believe the path to child abuse images begin. It has been theorized that individuals who engage in hours upon hours of viewing pornography will eventually become desensitized to what they see, causing them to search for more extreme images over time in order to satisfy an addictive rush they feel. For some, the hunt for the addictive rush leads to the realm of child sexual abuse images and, while they may know what they are viewing is illegal and morally wrong, it is the taboo nature of child pornography that keeps them coming back to chase the high they receive from viewing this material.

Another group of child pornography users are those who engage in child sexual abuse. Research has shown there is a strong link between watching child abuse material and physically sexually abusing children themselves. In a 2014 study, 57.5 percent of the research subjects who had been arrested for possession of child pornography also admitted to actual sexual child abuse[3]. When the study was replicated in 2016, the percentage had increased to 69 percent. A 2008 study reflected an even higher percentage. The researchers analyzed a population of sex offenders enrolled in a voluntary, prison-based treatment program. They found that the cross over between those who were charged with possession of child pornography and those who have sexually assaulted a child was 85 percent with an average of 13 victims per offender.[4] Another study by forensic psychologist Michael Seto, who is one of the world's leading researchers of pedophilia, found that 50 to 60 percent of consumers of child pornography also admit to sexually abusing children.[5]

Research has also highlighted that a person being abused themselves as a child can lead to the abusive relationships in their adult life. Researchers have stated that child sexual abuse may be used as a maladaptive coping mechanism for some, as it places them in place of power, thus overcoming the sense of powerlessness they felt when they were being abused themselves. Others may find themselves sexually aroused by abusive behavior especially if their early sexual experiences involved abuse. As child pornography is in fact images and videos of child sexual abuse, it is certainly conceivable that those who have been victims of sexual abuse themselves could be viewers and distributors of this type of imagery.

Regardless of why one may choose to download and view child pornography, the act of doing so is anything but a victimless crime. Child sexual abuse images are just that: images of the real sexual abuse of a child. The most horrendous moment of that child's life is being viewed for the sexual gratification of an adult. A child's knowledge that these images of themselves exist and are being circulated, creates a nexus of shame and embarrassment. And given that internet images are never fully erased from existence, that nexus is one that is never ending; revictimizing the child well into their adult years and for the remainder of their lives. The act of viewing child pornography creates a market for the material. Regardless of whether the viewer of child sexual abuse images and videos participates in the actual sexual abuse themselves, their views and downloads of this material creates the demand that producers of the child pornography are more than happy to supply. And as the market for this type of material grows, the sexual assault of children will not only continue, but will become more extreme and depraved to meet the repulsive tastes of its audience.

September 8th, 2020

It was late in the evening, and I was beaming with pride for making it to the gym that day. I pulled in my driveway when my phone rang, interrupting whatever song I was enjoying. It was one of my old law school colleagues. I sent her to voicemail. I needed a shower.

I could hear my phone ringing two more times over the running water. What could possibly be going on at this very moment that needed my attention. I stepped out of the shower, wrapping a towel around myself, and wiped the fog off my phone's screen. Both calls were from her. It must be important. I called her back, the phone ringing only once before she answered.

"He just pled guilty."

October 6th, 2020

For 10 months, his only ally was the woman who birthed him. While others saw him as vile, she saw her son. Strangers would go to his social media pages to voice their disgust with him.

"YOU SICK PERVERT!"

"YOU MAKE ME WANT TO THROW UP!"

"I HOPE YOU ROT IN HELL!"

The comments hurt her. She called those who made them cowards. She consistently urged people to remember that in America, you are innocent until proven guilty.

Well now he was just that; guilty. And the time for atonement had arrived.

Normally the steeple from my childhood church would greet me as I drove across the bridge into my hometown. But on this morning, the thick fog that set atop the town blocked everything not in my immediate vision from sight. I arrived at the courthouse at 8:30 and was greeted by the cool autumn air as I walked in the front door, past security and into the courtroom. At 8:40, two of the sheriffs were conversing. The more muscular of the two said he figured there would be more people in attendance. A few weeks prior, one of our classmates gleefully posted the date and time of his sentencing hearing. Some commenters replied that they would skip work to come. Others talked about bringing popcorn and bourbon.

But in the end, none of them showed up.

At 8:43, a slim man in a navy suit and red tie entered the courtroom and took his seat at the prosecutor's table. A moment later, a slightly older gentleman, clad in a light gray suit sat at the opposing defense table. Two of his law school accusers also entered. They sat behind me and lightly chatted about cases they were working on and the heavy fog that greeted them on the drive over. I knew they would feel that justice served in this case would be their long awaited justice as well.

At 9:00, the judge finally took her place at the center of the bench, in front of a mahogany-paneled wall with the huge gold state seal hanging above her head. She ordered for him to be brought in. My heart beat with anticipation.

Behind us, a door creaked open. I looked back and saw flashes of orange. From a back room, he emerged. When his mugshot was splattered on the news just 10 months ago, his hair was a dim brown, shortly cut and swooping over his forehead. But now, it was fully gray, long, slicked back, and descending to the base of his neck. 10 months ago, his shoulders were broad, his figure firm, and his orange jumpsuit baggy. But now, his midsection protruded, and his garb clung to him. As he walked down the aisle, the chains wrapped around his midsection and connecting to his hands rattled. He took his seat at the table.

Before the hearing, the details of his doings were scarce. The news stories gave us general headlines and his classmates speculated on Facebook. But today, we would learn the unsettling specifics. His ex-girlfriend told us about the rows of folders, named after the victims whose pictures were inside. Some of the names were those of children she knew. She told us of the threats of blackmail that made her uneasy to even be in court that day.

The lead detective in the case told us about the contents of the numerous thumb drives. He told us about the pictures of kids taken at the town park and the local Chick Fil La play area, with the camera zoomed in on the children's crotches and buttocks. He told us of future charges of child molestation that would soon be filed. He said it was the most disturbing case he had ever seen.

A member of the secret service told us that throughout all of the videos and pictures found, there were around 30,000 unique victims. We learned that there were pictures of kids he would take while he was hidden in the corners of his front porch and through the slightly parted blinds in his house. We learned about videos of him pleasuring himself in various places including our school's law library, his lawyer's office, and even in a judge's chambers. We learned that in the secret service agent's long career that included child pornography investigations on a national level, this was in his top three of the most disturbing and egregious cases.

While witness after witness were brought forth, I looked over at him. I have seen many defendants in the courtroom in my time. Many sit quietly in their chairs, letting their attorney do the work. In rare cases, some are vocally disruptive, having to be admonished by the judge. But he acted differently. He consistently leaned over to whisper long soliloquies in his attorney's ear. When he wasn't doing this, his pen was moving a mile a minute, taking notes with the furor of a brand-new law clerk. He didn't even look up when 22 of the most egregious videos from his collection were played in the courtroom. He just kept his head down, continuing to scribble notes. If it weren't for his orange jumpsuit, I would have confused him for his attorney's co-counsel.

When it was the defense's turn, a parade of family members and church friends were ushered into the courtroom, taking seats in the pews behind him. His mother took the stand first. I knew her face from her various comments on Facebook but I didn't realize the size of her presence until she was before me. She took the stand in her light gray sweater with the poise of a mother whose only job was to provide strength. Strength for her son. Strength for an entire family. From her we learned about his father. We learned how his father molested him and his sister. We learned that his father introduced him to pornography. She sat on the stand preaching the evil that his father brought upon their family with her congregation of family members nodding along, silently testifying to every word.

Other supporters would take the stand. His sister told us what he did wasn't shocking based on how they both grew up with. His aunt told us she had co-signed on his student loan and was worried about how she would tackle the $200,000 debt without him being able to work due to a long incarceration. His 16-year-old niece tearfully told us how he would help her with her science homework. Then her father, his brother-in-law, would tell us about their time spent chatting about football and cars. The brother-in-law chastised the media for "jumping to conclusions" and said he was a "good guy." I silently wondered how good of a guy he would be if pictures of the brother-in-law's 16-year-old daughter would have showed up on that iPad.

After the witness parade concluded, he took the stand. He had been trained in the law, just like us. He had dreams, just like us. And here he was in court, giving the only closing argument he would ever have the opportunity to give. He reminded us that he never once deflected responsibility and he accepts the evil he perpetrated. He harped on the fact that he had been cooperative. He told us the words "I'm sorry" failed to convey the amount of regret he truly had.

He begged for help.

He begged for mercy.

————

The begging and pleading ceased. The attorney monologues were done. It was time for the reckoning. The judge spoke. She acknowledged the harm his father did to him and his sister. She commended his sister for handling her healing with strength. She admonished him for inflicting the same harm he experienced as a child on others once he became an adult. She scolded him for downplaying the seriousness of his crimes, saying that the market for child abuse images is created by people like him; perpetuating the need for others to produce this material. She told him that despite being trained in the law, and knowing the law, he chose to continue breaking the law; a decades long practice he began when he started accumulating his child pornography collection in the mid-90s.

And then, her ruling.

Three charges of child exploitation with 10 year sentences a piece, to be served consecutively.

30 years total.

The gavel came down.

The family sobbed as they processed out of the courtroom.

And then a bailiff came to collect him.

Leading the monster in his chains, back to his cage.

[1] Some argue that referring to child sexual abuse imagery as pornography normalizes what is an incredibly heinous crime. While this argument is certainly acknowledged, as this is a legal based essay, the term "child pornography" shall be used as this is the term used in most state and Federal statutes.

[2] Wortley R. (2014) Child Pornography. In: Bruinsma G., Weisburd D. (eds) Encyclopedia of Criminology and Criminal Justice. Springer, New York, NY. https://doi.org/10.1007/978-1-4614-569 0-2_105.

[3] Michael L. Bourke, Lance Fragomeli, Paul J. Detar, Michael A. Sullivan, Edward Meyle & Mark O'Riordan (2015) The use of tactical polygraph with sex offenders, Journal of Sexual Aggression, 21:3, 354-367, DOI: 10.1080/13552600.2014.886729.

[4] Bourke, M.L., Hernandez, A.E. The 'Butner Study' Redux: A Report of the Incidence of Hands-on Child Victimization by Child Pornography Offenders. *J Fam Viol* 24, 183 (2009). https://doi.org/10.1007/s10896-008-9219-y.

[5] Seto MC, Karl Hanson R, Babchishin KM. Contact Sexual Offending by Men With Online Sexual Offenses. *Sexual Abuse.* 2011;23(1):124-145. doi:10.1177/1079063210369013.

17

REFERENCES

The Time I Got Banned for Writing About Fraternity Brothers Holding Each Other Accountable

- Knetbooks, https://blog.knetbooks.com

- Brandon Yamamoto, *5 Ways to Survive the Stress of College* (Dec. 18, 2017), https://blog.knetbooks.com/5-ways-to-su rvive-the-stressof-college/.

- Jenna Urusky, *Surviving as a Millennial with College Debt* (Nov. 16, 2018), https://blog.knetbooks.com/surviving-as -a-millennial-withcollege-debt/

- Joey Wilkerson, *The Off the Beaten Path Holiday Buying List for the College Gentleman* (Dec. 12, 2014), https://blog.knetbooks.com/off-beaten-path-holid ay-buying-list-college-gentleman/

- Joey Wilkerson, *Fall Fashion for Fellas – the Hoodie* (Oct. 8, 2014), https://blog.knetbooks.com/fall-fashion-fellas-hoo die/

- Ashley Collman, *University of Virginia Student Details Alleged Gang Rape by Seven Men During a Fraternity Initia tion... and Claims the School Did Nothing About It* (Nov. 21, 2014), https://www.dailymail.co.uk/news/article-284268 7/U-Va-asks-police-investigate-report-frat-house-rape.html

- CRIMESIDER STAFF, Wisc. College Frat Suspended over Date Rape Drug Allegations (Nov. 19, 2014), https://www.cbsnews.com/news/wisconsin-college -frat-suspended-over-date-rape-drug-allegations/

- *Brown University Student Tests Positive for Date-Rape Drug* (Nov. 10, 2014), https://abcnews.go.com/GMA/video/brown-univ ersitystudent-tests-positive-date-rape-drug-26805115

- Lucy Martinson, V Form, Taboo or Taking a Stand? Why Sexual Assault Needs More Attention (Apr. 24, 2018), https://smleo.com/2018/04/24/taboo-or-taking-a -stand-why-sexual-assault-needsmore-attention/

- *I've Talked with Teenage Boys About Sexual Assault for 20 Years. This Is What They Still Don't Know,* TIME, https://time.com/5503804/ive-talkedwith-teenage-boys-ab out-sexual-assault-for-20-years-this-is-whatthey-still-dont-k now/

- Mandy Van Deven, Why School Administrators Won't Talk About Sexual Harassment, NEWSWEEK (Nov. 17, 2014), https://www.newsweek.com/why-school-administ rators-wont-talk-about-sexual-harassment-84922

- Katie Baker, *Teaching Rape Law in the Age of the Trigger Warning*, BUZZFEED NEWS (Apr. 3, 2015), https://www.buzzfeednews.com/article/katiejmbaker/teaching-rape-law-in-the-age-of-the-triggerwarning

- Daniela Perez, *The Taboo on Sex Stems from Christian Values*, http://panthernow.com/2017/02/07/the-taboo-on-sex-stems-from-christian-values/

- *10 Surprising Health Benefits of Having Sex*, (Dec. 8, 2015), https://www.parhlo.com/health-benefits-of-sex/

- Abigail Fagan , *Why Is Sex So Taboo?*, PSYCHOLOGY TODAY (Apr. 9, 2011), https://www.psychologytoday.com/us/blog/the-big-questions/201104/why-is-sex-so-taboo

- Erin Mansur, *Taboo Topics: Sexual Assault*, THE DAILY NEBRASKAN (Mar. 16, 2015), http://www.dailynebraskan.com/culture/taboo-topicssexual-assault/article_da452a4c-cb8f-11e4-b594-576dd9383d43.html

- AMANDA FIELDER, *Why Is Sexual Assault More Taboo Than Domestic Violence?*, (Aug. 13, 2014), https://movingtoendsexualassault.org/sexual-assault-taboo-domestic-violence/

- National Lampoon's Animal House, Imdb, https://www.imdb.com/title/tt0077975/?ref_=fn_al_tt_1

- Emily DeLetter, *Purdue Fraternity Suspended After Student Accused of Rape in Clinton County*, JOURNAL & COURIER (Oct. 21, 2019),

https://www.jconline.com/story/news/2019/10/21/purdu
e-fraternitysuspended-after-student-accused-rape-clinton-c
ounty/4052302002/#

- Erin Gloria Ryan, *Infamous 'Rapebait' Frat Disband-ed for Being Entirely Too Rapey*, JEZEBEL (Apr. 4, 2014), https://jezebel.com/infamous-rape-bait-frat-disban ded-for-being-entirely-t-1558252895

- BARBARA BROSHER, *National Office Closes IU Chapter of Alpha Tau Omaga Fraternity*, (Oct. 8, 2015), https://www.wfyi.org/news/articles/national-office -closes-iu-chapter-of-alpha-tau-omaga-fraternity

- Mary Dowd, *How Hard Is the Pledging Process for a Frater-nity?*, SEATTLE PI,https://education.seattlepi.com/hard-p ledging-process-fraternity-3815.htm

- CHRISTINIA CRIPPES, *SigEp Fraternity 'See-Saws' Against Sexual Assault*, (Mar. 31, 2015), https://wcfcourier.com/news/local/education/sigep-fratern ity-see-saws-against-sexual-assault/article_762eac43-b7b4-5 422-9143-f7a02fa8e591.html

- Ashley Ahn, *To Improve Turnout at Education Pro-grams*, IFC Announces Harsher Sanctions for Fra-ternities, THE DAILY PENNSYLVANIAN (Feb. 12, 2019), https://www.thedp.com/article/2019/02/upenn-if c-fraternity-rush-new-member-education-recruitment

- Rebecca Ruiz, *How Do We Teach Frat Brothers Not to Rape?*, MASHABLE (Feb. 25, 2015), https://mashable.com/2015/

02/25/frats-campussexual-assault/

- Jill Deutsch, *MU Fraternity Members Are Teaching Each Other About Sexual Assault Prevention*, MISSOURIAN (Apr. 9, 2015), https://www.columbiamissourian.com/news/mu-fraternity -members-are-teaching-eachother-about-sexual-assault/arti cle_768d9d80-860a-5878-ab10-6ec54156374f.html

- Nsvrc, https://www.nsvrc.org/statistics

- *Interactive Games Help Address Drinking, Sexual Assault in College*, US NEWS (Aug. 18, 2015), https://www.usnews.com/education/best-colleges/articles/ 2015/08/18/interactive-games-help-address-drinkingsexual -assault-in-college

- Austin Faulds, *Greeks Speak Out Against Sexual Violence*, IDS NEWS (Apr. 28, 2016), https://www.idsnews.com/ar ticle/2016/04/greeks-speakout-against-sexual-violence

- Max Blau, *Washington State Fraternity Suspended Amid Sexual Assault Investigation*, CNN (Sept. 15, 2016), https://www.cnn.com/2016/09/15/us/washingto n-state-delta-upsilon-fraternity-suspension/index.html

- CAITLIN DOORNBOS, *Group of KU Greeks Form Task Force to Respond to Sexual Assault Allegations*, LJ WORLD (Oct. 3, 2014), https://www2.ljworld.com/news/2014/oc t/03/ku-greeks-respond-sexualassault-allegations/

- Samantha Tatro, Liberty Zabala & Lynn Walsh, *Three Fraternities Named in SDSU Reported Sex*

Assaults in 2014, NBC San Diego (Apr. 20, 2015), https://www.nbcsandiego.com/news/local/three-fr aternitiesnamed-in-sdsu-reported-sex-assaults/57894/

- Ron Wilkins, *Purdue Student Videoed Sexual Assault at Fraternity Party Off-Campus*, Prosecutors Say, Journal & Courier (Oct. 25, 2019), https://www.jconline.com/story/news/crime/2019/10/25/ purdue-studentallegedly-sexually-assaulted-woman-portabl e-restroom/2454443001/

- Grace Elizabeth O'Brien, *Why Sexual Assault Education Is Important to Everyone*, (Apr. 21, 2016), https://www.theo dysseyonline.com/sexualassault-important-everyone

Extracurricular Activities: The Fetishization of Female Defendants in Sexual Misconduct Cases

- John P. Wise & Connie Leonard, T*rinity HS Teacher, Coach Facing Federal Child Porn Charges*, WAVE 3 NEWS (June 2, 2015), https://www.wave3.com/story/29221193/trinity-h s-teacher-coach-facing-federalchild-porn-charges/

- *Former Trinity High School Teacher Sentenced to 42 Years for Child Porn Charges*, WDRB (Jan. 6, 2016), https://www.wdrb.com/news/crimereports/former-trinity -high-school-teacher-sentenced-to-42-yearsfor-child-porn-c harges/article_c4c1065c-0ac1-5a95-9cbdafb340a44269.ht ml#:~:text=%28WDRB%29%20--%20A%20-former%20Tri nity%20High%20School%20teacher,charges.%20Last%20s ummer%2C%20Patrick%20Newman%3.

- *Fired Trinity High School Teacher and Coach Patrick Newman Exploited 16 Boys to Produce Child Pornography.*, FACEBOOK -- COURIER JOURNAL (Jan. 6,2016), https://www.facebook.com/courierjournal/posts /10153187009476993.

- Lauren Fruen, *Former Miss Kentucky Beauty Queen, 28, Arrested for 'Sending Nude Photos to 15-Year-Old Boy on Snapchat*, THE SUN (Dec. 9, 2018), https://www.thesun.co.uk/news/worldnews/7934788/for mer-miss-kentucky-beauty-queen-ramsey-bearse-arrested-n udephotos-student-snapchat/.

- Allen Kim, *Former Miss Kentucky Sentenced to 2 Years in Prison for Sending Topless Photos to a 15-Year-Old Student*, CNN (July 17, 2020), https://www.cnn.com/2020/07/17 /us/miss-kentucky-ramsey-bearse-trnd/index.html

- USA TODAY (July 18, 2020), https://www.facebook.com/usatoday/posts/ramsey-bethan n-bearse-29-admitted-to-exchanging-sexualphotos-with-a-t eenage-stu/10158607818675667/

- South Park Studios, Miss Teacher Bangs a Boy - SOUTH PARK, YouTube (Sept. 3, 2015), https://www.youtube.c om/watch?v=h7SpXGz-XOc

- Hollie McKay, *Female Teachers Having Sex with Students: Double Standards, Lack of Awareness*, FOX NEWS, https://www.foxnews.com/us/femaleteachers-hav

ing-sex-with-students-double-standards-lack-of-awareness.

• Amanda Garrett, *More Female Teachers Caught Having Sex with Students, Experts Say*, THE COLUMBUS DISPATCH (June 3, 2019), https://www.dispatch.com/news/20190603/more-female-teachers-caughthaving-sex-with-students-experts-say.

• William Moore, *Double Standard: Female Sex Offenders Can Get 'Sweetheart Deals'*, SUN HERALD (Apr. 17, 2016), https://www.sunherald.com/news/local/crime/article72339207.html

• Connor Mannion, *Recently Divorced Teacher Allegedly Sexually Assaulted Student and Sent Explicit Videos to Another*, OXYGEN (July 14, 2020), https://www.oxygen.com/crime-news/kentucky-teachermollie-verkamp-charged-rape-teen-student.

• Jerry Thornton, *2018 Sex Scandal Teacher Starting Lineup*, BARSTOOL SPORTS (Jan. 2, 2019), https://www.barstoolsports.com/blog/1181156/2018-sex-scandal-teacher-starting-lineup.

• MulaMovieClips, *American Pie (1999) Stifler's Mom*, YouTube (Mar. 14, 2020), https://www.youtube.com/watch?v=o9Q7iSj_QdQ.

• https://blog.redtube.com/2017/09/hot-for-teacher/

• True Crime Daily, https://truecrimedaily.com

• JCS - Criminal Psychology, *Jennifer's Solution*, YouTube

(Sept. 3, 2020), https://www.youtube.com/watch?v=UQt
46gvYO40.

- Teacher Sex Offender List: 25 Female Teacher and Student
  Sex Crime Scandals, LAWFIRMS, https://www.lawfirms.co
  m/female-teacher-sex-crimeoffenders-and-scandals.htm.

- *Double Standard Seen When Boys Abused by Women*, USA
  TODAY   (Nov.   18,   2013),
  https://www.usatoday.com/story/news/nation/2013/11/1
  8/double-standard-seen-when-boys-sexually-abused-by-wo
  men/3615947/.

- William Moore, *E Sex Offenders Can Get 'Sweetheart Deals'*,
  SUN HERALD (Apr. 17, 2016)

- Greg   Kocher,   *Ex-Educator   in   Woodford,   Fayette
  Gets   18-Month   Sentence   for   Student   Rape,
  Sodomy*, https://www.kentucky.com/news/local/crime/a
  rticle222674485.html#storylink=cpy, Lexington Herald
  Leader (Dec. 5, 2018)

- FOX 19, https://www.fox19.com/story/19223617/andrea
  -connerssentenced-for-sex-with-highlands-hs-student/

- Bill Robinson, *Ex-Teacher Gets One-Year on Sex Charge*,
  RICHMOND   REGISTER   (Jan.   30,   2017),
  https://www.richmondregister.com/news/ex-teacher-gets-o
  ne-year-on-sex-charge/article_5448e3fc-e71c-11e6-bd01-17
  3600c75a2c.html

- Sebastian Murdock, *Judge Gives Teacher Who Had Sex
  with Student 30 Days, Calls Her 'Dangling Candy'*, HUFF-

POST, https://www.huffpost.com/entry/teacher-sex-30-da ys-candy_n_7006672.

- Barbara Goldberg, *U.S. Cracks Down on Female Teachers Who Sexually Abuse Students*, REUTERS (Apr. 21, 2015), https://www.reuters.com/article/us-usa-crime-teac hers-idUSKBN0NC14H20150421.

- Brian Dakss, *Sparks Fly in Teacher Sex Case*, CBS NEWS (Nov. 22, 2005).

- Charles Montaldo, *The Debra Lafave Case*, THOUGHTCO (Oct. 24, 2019), https://www.thoughtco.com/debra-lafave -case-971065.

- Debra Lafave, *Teacher Convicted of Sex with Student, Ordered Back on Probation*, TAMPA BAY TIMES (Aug. 16, 2 0 1 2) , https://www.tampabay.com/news/courts/debra-lafave-teac her-convicted-of-sex-withstudent-ordered-back-on/124597 8/

- Suzanne Goldenberg, *Too Pretty for Prison*, THE GUARDIAN (Mar. 23,2006), https://www.theguardian.com/world/20 06/mar/24/usa.gender

- Matthew Santoni, *Ex-Plum Teacher Pleads Guilty, Sentenced to Prison for Sex with Student*, TRIBLIVE (Apr. 18, 2 0 1 6) , https://archive.triblive.com/local/pittsburgh-allegheny/ex -plum-teacher-pleadsguilty-sentenced-to-prison-for-sex-wit h-student/.

- https://scallywagandvagabond.com/2020/07/ramsey-betha nnbearse-sentenced-former-miss-kentucky-illicit-photos-tee n-boy/.

Yeezy Taught Me: Kanye West and the Characteristics of Abuse

- Diana Dasrath & David K. Li, *Kim Kardashian Files for Divorce from Kanye West*, NBC NEWS (Feb. 20, 2021, 9:42 A M) , https://www.nbcnews.com/news/us-news/kim-kardashian -files-divorce-kanye-west-n1258382?cid=sm_npd_nn_tw_ ma.

- Leah Bitsky, *Kim Kardashian Slams Kanye West's 'Obsession' with 'Attacking' her Amid Divorce*, PAGE SIX (Feb. 4, 2022, 11:07AM), https://pagesix.com/2022/02/04/kim-kardashian-slams-ka nye-west-for-trying-to-control-and-manipulate-divorce/.

- *Domestic Violence*, Office on Violence Against Women (OVW), https://www.justice.gov/ovw/domestic-violence.

- Tiffany White, *Kim, Sweetheart, It's Time to Stop Letting Kanye West Tell You What to Wear*, LIFE & STYLE (Jan 11, 2018, 2:27 PM), https://www.lifeand-stylemag.com/posts/kanye-west-controlling-151108/.

Joanna Crawly, *Kim Kardashian Reveals Kanye West Told Her She Had 'the Worst Style' and Admits She Cried When Her Husband Cleaned Out Her Closet*, DAILY MAIL (Jun.

20,   2018),
https://www.dailymail.co.uk/tvshowbiz/article-5864799/
Kim-Kardashian-reveals-husband-Kanye-West-told-worse-st
yle.html.

- Sam Reed, *How Will Kim Kardashian Dress Without Kanye Controlling Her Closet?*, INSTYLE (Jan. 6, 2021), https://www.instyle.com/celebrity/kim-kardashian -style-post-kanye.

- Sophie Goddard, *10 Ways to Spot Coercive Control*, COSMOPOLITAN (Jul. 24, 2018), https://www.cosmopolitan.com/uk/reports/news/a31487/what-is-coercive-control/.

- Caity Weaver, *Kim Kardashian West on Kanye and Taylor Swift, What's in O.J.'s Bag, and Understanding Caitlyn*, GQ (Jun. 16, 2016), https://www.gq.com/story/kim-kardashia n-west-gq-cover-story.

- *Fox News*, INTERVIEW (Jan. 15, 2022), https://www.inter viewmagazine.com/culture/fox-news.

- Hope Schreiber, *New Neighbors? Kim Kardashian Is 'Not Thrilled' About Kanye West Moving Across the Street*, INTOUCH (Dec 31, 2021, 12:54 PM), https://www.intouchweekly.com/posts/kim-kardas hian-not-thrilled-kanye-west-moving-across-street/.

- Timothy J. Legg, *How to Recognize Coercive Control*, HEALTHLINE (Oct. 10, 2019), https://www.healthline.co m/health/coercive-control.

- *Kanye West Claims Pete Davidson Has AIDS; Twitter Says*

Rumor is 'Grotesque' & 'Abuse', BLAST (Jan. 28, 2022, 11:29 A   M   )   , https://theblast.com/167938/kanye-west-claims-pete-david-son-has-aids-twitter-says-rumor-is-grotesque-abuse/.

Jessica Bennett, *Kanye West Cuts Kid Cudi from Album Over Friendship with Pete Davidson*, PAGE SIX (Feb. 13, 2022,   10:38AM), https://pagesix.com/2022/02/13/kanye-west-cuts-kid-cudi -from-album-over-friendship-with-pete-davidson/.

- Jessica Bennett, *Kanye West Continues to Bash 'd–khead' Pete Davidson*, PAGE SIX (Feb. 13, 2022, 12:28PM), https://pagesix.com/2022/02/13/kanye-west-c ontinues-to-bash-d-khead-pete-davidson/.

- Adam S. Levy, Christine Rendon, & Cassie Carpenter, *'Why can't you keep any of our conversations private?' Kanye West shares angry texts sent to him by ex-Kim Kardashian before he then DELETES his Instagram except for pictures of her with their kids*, DAILYMAIL (Feb. 14, 2022), https://www.dailymail.co.uk/tvshowbiz/article-10513165/ Kim-Kardashian-texts-Kanye-Ye-West-asks-stop-putting-Pet e-Davidson-danger.html.

- Michael Schreiner, *Abusers Try To Shift The Blame To Become The 'Victims'*, EVOLUTION COUNSELING (Jun. 29, 2017), https://evolutioncounseling.com/abusers-try-to-shi ft-the-blame-to-become-the-victims/.

- *National Statistics*, NCADV, https://ncadv.org/statistics.

Attorneys Say the Darndest Things

- Ginger Adam Otis, *Donald Trump Lawyer Says 'You cannot Rape Your Spouse,' Claims There is 'Very Clear Case Law' to Prove it Can't be Rape: Report*, DAILY NEWS (Jul. 28, 2015, 10:47 AM), https://www.nydailynews.com/2015/07/28/donald-trump -lawyer-says-you-cannot-rape-your-spouse-claims-there-is-v ery-clear-case-law-to-prove-it-cant-be-rape-report/.

- § 2.13.1. Rape and Related Offenses, Model Penal Code § 2.13.1.

- Laura Bates, *Yes, There is Such a Thing as Rape Within Marriage*, THE GUARDIAN (Jul. 29, 2015), https://www.theguardian.com/lifeandstyle/womens-blog/ 2015/jul/29/yes-there-is-such-a-thing-as-within-marriage.

- Laura Bradley, *Cuba Gooding Jr. Now Faces Unwanted Touching Accusations From 22 Women*, VANITY FAIR (Dec. 10, 2019), https://www.vanityfair.com/hollywood/2019/ 12/cuba-gooding-jr-groping-allegations.

- Joe Price, *Cuba Gooding Jr. Is Facing Groping Accusations From 30 Women, Prosecutors Say (UPDATE)*, COMPLEX (Aug. 14, 2020), https://www.complex.com/pop-culture/a/backwoodsaltar/ cuba-gooding-jr-facing-groping-accusations-from-30-wome n.

- Laura Bradley, *Cuba Gooding Jr.'s Lawyer Says Small Boobs*

Can Make Women Delusional About Sexual Assault, DAILY
BEAST   (Aug.   13,   2020, 4:15PM),
https://www.thedailybeast.com/cuba-gooding-jrs-lawyer-sa
ys-small-boobs-can-make-women-delusional-about-sexual-a
ssault.

• Molly Redden, *Five Other Politicians Who've Said Id-
iotic Things About Rape*, THE REPUBLIC (Aug, 20,
2012), https://newrepublic.com/article/106317/five-othe
r-politicians-whove-said-idiotic-things-about-rape.

• *The Medieval Wing of the Republican Party*, POLITICS WEST CHESTER REVIEW (Sept. 2,
2012), https://politicswestchestereview.wordpress.com/20
12/09/02/those-medieval-republicans/.

• Maisha Johnson, *Is Outercourse the Same Thing as Ab-
stinence? And 5 Other Questions, Answered*, HEALTHLINE
(Mar. 8, 2019), https://www.healthine.com/health-sex/ou
tercourse.

Please Don't Share These: A Revenge Porn Primer

• Emma Grey Ellis, *It's Time for Facebook to Deal With the
Grimy History of Revenge Porn*, WIRED (Mar. 14, 2017, 4:49
PM), https://www.wired.com/2017/03/revenge-porn-face
book/.

• What is Revenge Porn?, PSYCH CENTRAL (Feb. 11, 2018),
https://psychcentral.com/blog/what-is-revenge-porn#1.

- *Civil Rights Initiative*, https://cybercivilrights.org/

- Gabrielle Fonrouge, *Inside the Twisted Revenge Porn Site That's Ruining Women's Lives*, NEW YORK POST (Sept. 22, 2017, 12:14 AM), https://nypost.com/2017/09/22/reven ge-porn-site-leaves-trail-of-innocent-victims/.

- Lori Janjigian, *Nearly 10 Million Americans are Victims of Revenge Porn, Study Finds*, BUSINESS INSIDER (Dec 13, 2016, 5:03 PM), https://www.businessinsider.com/revenge-porn-stu dy-nearly-10-million-americans-are-victims-2016-12.

- Madeline Buxton, *For Survivors Of Revenge Porn, The Fight To Enact Laws Continues*, REFINERY29 (Sept. 27, 2018, 5:10 PM), https://www.refinery29.com/en-us/2018/09/20997 4/nonconsensual-image-sharing-real-life-stories.

- Gabrielle Fonrouge, *Revenge Porn Nearly Ruined my Life*, NEW YORK POST (Nov. 16, 2017, 2:56 PM), https://nypo st.com/2017/11/16/revenge-porn-nearly-ruined-my-life/.

- Sophia Ankel, *'The Damage She Caused was Irreversible': 90% of Male Revenge Porn Victims are Also Blackmailed, but the Police Just Don't Care*, BUSINESS INSIDER (Apr 26, 2020, 5:46 AM), https://www.businessinsider.com/90-pe rcent-of-male-revenge-porn-victims-blackmail-2020-4.

- Research Reveals Gendered Trends in Revenge Porn Crimes, SWGFL (Aug. 23, 2019), https://swgfl.org.uk/magazine/r evenge-porn-research-2019/.

- David Cornell, *Jennifer Lawrence On 'The Fap-*

pening': *'It's A Sex Crime'*, INQUISTR (Oct. 3, 2014), https://www.inquisitr.com/1524579/jennifer-lawr ence-the-fappening-sex-crime.

* Jake Burns, *Ex Hanover Special Ed Teacher Pleads Guilty in "Celebgate" Hacking Scandal*, RICHMOND NEWS 6 (Oct 22, 2 0 1 8) , https://www.wtvr.com/2018/10/22/former-richmond-spe cial-ed-teacher-pleads-guilty-in-celebgate-hacking-scandal.

* Thomas James Brennan, *Hundreds of Marines Investigated for Sharing Photos of Naked Colleagues*, REVEAL (Mar. 4, 2017), https://revealnews.org/blog/hundreds-of-marines-i nvestigated-for-sharing-photos-of-naked-colleagues/.

* Jeff Schogol, *'I Don't Want to Leave my House': Victims Haunted by Marines' Nude Photo Scandal*, MARINE CORPS TIMES (Mar. 6, 2017), https://www.marinecorpstimes.com/news/pentagon-congr ess/2017/03/06/i-don-t-want-to-leave-my-house-victims-h aunted-by-marines-nude-photo-scandal/.

* Matthew Gault, *Police Have Seized Revenge Porn Site Anon-IB*, VICE (Apr. 25, 2018, 12:46 PM), https://www.vice.com/en/article/mbxdwv/anon-ib-r evenge-porn-site-seized-by-politie.

* Mike Mosedale, *Why Can't Minnesota Prosecute "Re- venge Porn" Harassment?*, MPLS ST. PAUL (Apr. 20, 2020), https://mspmag.com/arts-and-culture/minnesota-r evenge-porn-harassment/.

222   JAMES J. WILKERSON

- Steve Karnowski, *Court of Appeals Strikes Down Minnesota's Revenge Porn Law*, AP (Dec. 23, 2019), https://apnews.co m/general-news-210b1a8fb39718e634c42817462859a3.

- Mike Marturello, *Indiana's Revenge Porn Law Ruled Unconstitutional in Steuben Case*, THE HERALD REPUBLICAN (Nov. 6, 2020), https://www.kpcnews.com/heraldrepublic an/article_d67bfc4b-6dec-5d62-bf53-5d8b57b63590.html.

- Elizaberh Nolan Brown, *Law Prohibiting 'Revenge Porn' Violates First Amendment, Says Texas Appeals Court*, REASON (Apr. 28, 2018), https://reason.com/2018/04/23/texas-re venge-porn/.

- H.B. 98, 2019 Leg., 86th Sess. (Tx. 2019).

- H.R. 4472, 115 Cong. (1st Sess. 2017).

- Jenn Selby, *Lena Dunham on Nude 4Chan Photo Leaks: 'Hackers are Sex Offenders'*, INDEPENDENT (Sept. 3, 2014), https://www.independent.co.uk/news/people/lena-dunha m-on-nude-4chan-photo-leaks-hackers-are-sex-offenders-97 05672.html.

Fruit of the Poisonous Tree: How Toxic Masculinity Produces Sexual Assault

- Jon Johnson, *What to Know About Toxic Masculinity*, MEDICAL NEWS TODAY (Jun. 21, 2020), https://www.m edicalnewstoday.com/articles/toxicmasculinity.

- *Harmful Masculinity and Violence*, AMERICAN PSYCHO-

LOGICAL ASSOCIATION, https://www.apa.org/pi/about/
newsletter/2018/09/harmful-masculinity.

- Patrick Verel, *To Fight Toxic Masculinity, Look to Sources of
  Entitlement, Says Professor*, FORDHAM NEWS (Jan. 23,
  2   0   1   9   )   ,
  https://news.fordham.edu/politics-and-society/to-fight-tox
  ic-masculinity-look-to-sources-of-entitlement-say-professor
  /.

- Rachel Janik, *"I Laugh at the Death or Normies": How Incels
  Are Celebrating the Toronto Mass Killing*, SOUTHERN
  POVERTY   LAW   CENTER   (Apr.   24,   2018),
  https://www.splcenter.org/hatewatch/2018/04/24/i-laugh
  -death-normies-how-incels-are-celebrating-toronto-mass-kil
  ling.

- Peter Baker, *The Woman Who Accidentally Started the Incel
  Movement*, ELLE (Mar. 1, 2016), https://www.elle.com/cu
  lture/news/a34512/woman-who-started-incel-movement/.

- Sarah Mervosh, *New Baylor Lawsuit Alleges 52 Rapes by
  Football Players in 4 Years, 'Show 'Em a Good Time Culture*,
  THE DALLAS MORNING NEWS (Jan. 27, 2017),
  https://www.dallasnews.com/news/2017/01/27/new-bayl
  or-lawsuit-alleges-52-rapes-by-football-players-in-4-years-sh
  ow-em-a-good-time-culture/.

- Kyle Boone. *Louisville to Vacate 2013 National Title, Take
  Banner Down After NCAA Upholds Penalties*, CBS (Feb. 20,
  2018,   12:14   PM),
  https://www.cbssports.com/college-basketball/news/louisv

ille-to-vacate-2013-national-title-take-banner-down-after-n
caa-upholds-penalties/.

The New New Nine: Title IX Changes Through Two Vastly Different Administrations

- 20 U.S.C. §1681-§1688.

- *Dear Colleague Letter*, U.S. DEPARTMENT OF EDUCATION (Apr. 4, 2011), https://www2.ed.gov/about/offices/list/oc r/letters/colleague-201104.html.

- *Betsy DeVos Is Going To End Obama Rules on Campus Sex Assault*, COSMOPOLITAN (Sept. 7th, 2017), https://www.cosmopolitan.com/politics/a12193201/betsy -devos-is-going-to-end-obama-rules-on-campus-sex-assault/
.

- Robbie Soave, *Betsy DeVos Withdraws 'Dear Colleague' Letter That Weaponized Title IX Against Due Process*, REASON (Sept. 22, 2017), https://reason.com/2017/09/22/breakin g-betsy-devos-withdraws-dear-coll/.

- Casey Mendoza, *Betsy DeVos Plans To Overhaul 'Failed' Title IX Policies*, SCRIPPS NEWS (Sept. 7, 2017), https://scrippsnews.com/stories/betsy-devos-just-a nnounced-plans-to-change-title-ix-policies/.

- Greta Anderson, U.S. Publishes New Regulations on Campus Sexual Assault, INSIDE HIGHER ED (May 7, 2020), https://www.insidehighered.com/news/2020/05/0

7/education-department-releases-final-title-ix-regulations.

- *Title IX Regulations Addressing Sexual Harassment* (Unofficial Copy), U.S. DEPARTMENT OF EDUCATION, https://www2.ed.gov/about/offices/list/ocr/docs/titleix-regs-unofficial.pdf (last visited May 18, 2020).

- Sarah Brown, *How Professors Have to Report Sexual Misconduct. How Should They Tell Their Students That?*, THE CHRONICLE OF HIGHER EDUCATION (Aug. 16, 2108), https://www.chronicle.com/article/Many-Professors-Have-to-Report/244294/.

- Andrew Kreighbaum, *New Uncertainty on Title IX*, INSIDE HIGHER ED (Nov. 20, 2018), https://www.insidehighered.com/news/2018/11/20/title-ix-rules-cross-examination-would-make-colleges-act-courts-lawyers-say.

- *Joe Biden is responsible for the Violence Against Women Act: Day 13 of 100 days of loving Joe Biden*, DAILY KOS (Jul. 17, 2020), https://www.dailykos.com/stories/2020/7/17/1958845/-Joe-Biden-is-responsible-for-the-Violence-Against-Women-Act-Day-13-of-100-days-of-loving-Joe-Biden.

- Travis Waldron, *How Obama Took An Existing Feminist Law And Made It Even Stronger*, HUFFINGTON POST (Jan. 7, 2017), https://www.huffpost.com/entry/obama-title-ix_n_585afcd5e4b0eb5864851a93.

- Tyler Kingkade, *Obama Administration Warns*

Schools To Allow Transgender Access To Bathrooms, HUFFINGTON POST (May 13, 2016), https://www.huffpost.com/entry/obama-transgend er-bathrooms_n_57353d73e4b060aa7819eea4.

- Bianca Quilantan, *Biden Vows Quick End to DeVos' Sexual Misconduct Rule*, POLITCO (May 6, 2020), https://www.politico.com/news/2020/05/06/biden-vows -a-quick-end-to-devos-sexual-misconduct-rule-241715.

What I Learned About Sexual Assault Education in Higher Education from NASPA

- *The Importance of Theory in Research*, RESEARCH O'MAT-IC, https://www.researchomatic.com/the-importance-of-t heory-in-research-196282.html.

- *8 Tips for Integrating Pop Culture in the Classroom*, TEACH THOUGHT (Mar. 10, 2013), https://www.teachthought.com/pedagogy/8-tips-f or-integrating-pop-culture-in-the-classroom/.

- Siddhi Kamble, *How Different Generations Use Social Media*, FEED DOUGH (July 28, 2023), https://www.feedough .com/how-different-generations-use-social-media/.

- *Beyond Millennials: The Next Generation of Learners*, GLOBAL RESEARCH & INSIGHTS (Aug. 2018), https://www.pearson.com/content/dam/one-dot-c om/one-dot-com/global/Files/news/news-annoucements/ 2018/The-Next-Generation-of-Learners_final.pdf.

- Christopher Koulouris, *Integrating Pop Culture in Education: Engaging Students and Continued Interest in Learning. Incorporating Wider Culture as an Educational Tool.*, SCALLYWAG AND VAGABOND (Sept. 3, 2020), https://scallywagandvagabond.com/2020/09/7-ways-to-in corporate-pop-culture-in-education/#google_vignette.

- Kendra Cherry, *The Diffusion of Responsibility Concept in Psychology, The Diffusion of Responsibility Concept in Psychology*, VERY MIND WELL (Aug. 10, 2023), https://www.verywellmind.com/what-is-diffusion -of-responsibility-2795095.

- *Gender-Based Violence (Violence Against Women and Girls)*, The World Bank (Sept. 25, 2019), https://www.worldbank.org/en/topic/socialsustain ability/brief/violence-against-women-and-girls.

- Tupac Shakur 1988 High School Interview, YOUTUBE, ht tps://youtu.be/v_XT9-C5Qu8?si=e9THBqkP05vjTqxF.

- Jessica Valenti, *Frat Brothers Rape 300% More. One in 5 Women is Sexually Assaulted on Campus. Should we Ban Frats*, THE GUARDIAN (Sept. 24, 2014), https://www.theguardian.com/commentisfree/201 4/sep/24/rape-sexual-assault-ban-frats.

- Nina Friend, *Women Don't Feel As Safe As Men On College Campuses, Survey Shows*, HUFFINGTON POST (Jun. 26, 2014), https://www.huffpost.com/entry/women-safe-on-c ampus_n_5534267.

- Allie Bidwell, *Campus Sexual Assault: More Awareness Hasn't Solved Root Issues*, U.S. NEWS AND WORLD REPORT (May 20, 2015), https://www.usnews.com/news/articles/2015/05/20/sexua l-assault-on-college-campuses-more-awareness-hasnt-solved -underlying-issues.

- Carl Boisrond, *If Your Teacher Looks Like You, You May Do Better In School*, NPR ED (Sept. 29, 2017), https://www.npr.org/sections/ed/2017/09/29/552929074 /if-your-teacher-looks-likes-you-you-may-do-better-in-scho ol.

- Gabriel Fisher, *Study: Girls Do Better in School When Taught by Women*, QUARTZ (Jul. 31, 2015), https://qz.com/4662 46/study-girls-do-better-in-school-when-taught-by-women.

Cosby, Kelly, and Racial Injustice in Sexual Assault Cases

- *Bill Cosby Formally Charged with Felony Sexual Assault*, FOX 40 (Dec. 30, 2015, 7:19 AM), https://fox40.com/news/entertainment/pennsylvan ia-da-to-announce-if-bill-cosby-will-face-charges/.

- Timeline: Bill Cosby: A 50-Year Chronicle of Accusations and Accomplishments, LOS ANGELES TIMES (Sept. 28, 2018. 11:34 AM), https://www.latimes.com/entertainmen t/la-et-bill-cosby-timeline-htmlstory.html.

- Holly Yan, et al., *Bill Cosby Admitted to Getting Quaaludes to Give to Women*, CNN (Jul. 7, 2015, 11:42 PM), https:/

/www.cnn.com/allegations/index.html.

- Anastasia Tsioulcas, *R. Kelly Paid Bribe So He Could Marry 15-Year-Old Aaliyah, Government Alleges*, NPR (Dec. 5, 2019, 9:34   PM), https://www.npr.org/2019/12/05/785356513/rkelly-bribe-official-to-marry-15-year-old-aaliyah-government-alleges.

- Stacy St. Clair & Kayce T. Ataiyero, *Why the Jury Acquitted R. Kelly*, CHICAGO TRIBUNE (Jun. 14, 2008), https://www.chicagotribune.com/news/ct-xpm-20 08-06-14-0806140185-story.html.

- Sara Snider, *CNN Has Seen Tape Avenatti Says Shows R. Kelly Having Sex With Underage Girl*, CNN (Feb. 24, 2019, 6:55 PM), https://www.cnn.com/2019/02/14/entertainm ent/r-kelly-investigation/index.html.

- Carma Henry, *The Truth About Bill Cosby, R. Kelly, and America's War Against Black Masculinity*, WESTSIDE GAZETTE   (Jan.   29,   2020), https://thewestsidegazette.com/the-truth-about-bill-cosby -r-kelly-and-americas-war-against-black-masculinity/.

- Christopher Ingraham, *Black Men Sentenced to More Time for Committing the Exact Same Crime as a White Person, Study Finds*, WASHINGTON POST (Nov. 16, 2017, 1:33 P   M   )   , https://www.washingtonpost.com/news/wonk/wp/2017/ 11/16/black-men-sentenced-to-more-time-for-committing -the-exact-same-crime-as-a-white-person-study-finds/.

- Justin Wolfers, et al. *1.5 Million Missing Black Men*, NEW YORK TIMES (Apr. 20. 2015), https://www.nytimes.com/interacctive/2015/04/20/upshot/missing-black-men.html.

- Tara Culp-Ressler, *Why Stop and Frisk Could Be Bad for Americans' Health*, THINK PROGRESS (Oct. 17, 2014, 1:24 PM), https://archive.thingprogress.org/why-stop-and-frisk-could-be-bad-for-americans-health-ca403b384520/.

- Edwin Grimsley, *African American Wrongful Convictions Throughout History*, INNOCENCE PROJECT (Feb. 28, 2013), https://innocenceproject.org/african-american-wrongful-convictions-throught-history/.

- *The Central Park Five*, HISTORY (Sept. 23, 2019), https://www.history.com/topics/1089s/central-park-five.

- Eric Ortiz, *Groveland Four, the Black Men Pardoned After 1949 Rape Accusation, Honored with Memorial*, NBC NEWS (Feb. 21, 2020, 7:04 PM), https://www.nbcnews.com/news/us-news/groveland-four-black-men-pardoned-after-1949-rape-accusation-honored-m1140556.

- Meghan Keneally, *Man Exonerated Over Wrongful Rape Convection After 36 Years in Prison*, ABC NEWS (Mar. 22, 2019, 12:41 PM), https://abcnews.go.com/US/man-exonerated-over-wrongful-rape-convection-after-36-years-in-prison/story?id=61865415.

- John Maki, *Barney Brown: His First Year of Freedom*, HUFF-

INGTON POST (Dec. 6, 2017), https://www.huffpost.com
/entry/barney-brown-his-ye_b_297837.

• *The Murder of Emmitt Till*, PBS, https://www.pbs.org/w
gbh/americanexperience/features/till-timeline/.

Politicians Say the Darndest Things

• *Rape-Kit Remarks Put Rep. Jodie Laubenberg of Collin
County in Spotlight*, DALLAS MORNING NEWS (Jun. 25,
2013,   10:10   PM)
https://www.dallasnews.com/news/politics/2013/06/26/ra
pe-kit-remarks-put-rep-jodie-laubenberg-of-collin-county-i
n-spotlight/.

• Jessica Ravitz, *The Story Behind the First Rape Kit*, CNN
(Nov. 21, 2015, 10:29 PM), https://www.cnn.com/2015/
11/20/health/rape-kit-history/index.html.

• S.B. 150, 16 Reg. Sess. (Ky. 2016).

• Chris Williams, *Arrestee DNA Bill Narrowly Passes
Kentucky Senate Committee*, WHAS 11 (Mar. 10, 2016, 9:21
P   M   )   ,
https://www.whas11.com/article/news/politics/arrestee-dn
a-bill-narrowly-passes-kentucky-senate-committee/417-767
69003.

• *Katie Sepich- Katie's Law*, CRIMINAL DISCOURSE POD-
CAST (Jan. 4, 2021), https://criminaldiscoursepodcast.com
/katie-sepich/.

- *Convicted Child Rapist Micah Schoettle Sentenced to 23 Years in Prison*, WCPO (Aug. 5, 2018), https://www.wcpo.com/news/crime/convicted-child-rapist-micah-schoettle-sentenced-to-23-years-in-prison.

- Brakkton Booker, *Ex-Kentucky Gov. Defends Controversial Pardons for Child Rapist, Murderer*, NPR (Dec. 20, 2019, 1:34 PM), https:/www.npr.org/2019/12/20/790182205/ex-kentucky-gov-defends-controversial-pardons-for-child-rapist-murderer.

- *Rapper T.I. Faces Major Backlash for 'Hymen' Comments*, ABC NEWS (Nov. 7, 2019, 3:21 PM), https://abcnews.go.com/Lifestyle/wireStory/rapper-ti-faces-major-backlash-for-hymen-comments-66828708.

How Bad Do You Want In?

- *25 Interesting Facts About Hazing*, INSIDE HAZING, https://www.insidehazing.com/statistics.

- Katie Reilly, *College Students Keep Dying Because of Fraternity Hazing. Why Is It So Hard to Stop?*, TIME, https://time.com/4976836/fraternity-hazing-deaths-reform-tim-piazza/.

- *Hazing Policy*, DARTMOUTH, https://student-affairs.dartmouth.edu/policy/hazing-policy.

- *Sexual Assaults in High School Sports Minimized as "Hazing"*, CBS NEWS (May 8, 2017, 11:16

AM), https://www.cbsnews.com/news/sexual-assaults-in -high-school-sports-minimized-as-hazing-ap/.

- C. Todd Lopez, *Male Hazing Most Common Type of Sexual Assault, Expert Reveals*, U.S. ARMY (Apr. 18, 2016), https://www.army.mil/article/166188/male_hazin g_most_common_type_of_sexual_assault_expert_reveals.

- Jeckell A.S., Copenhaver E.A., Diamond A.B. *The spectrum of hazing and peer sexual abuse in sports: A current perspective*. SPORTS HEALTH. 2018;**10**:558–564. doi: 10.1177/1 941738118797322.

- Rebecca Onion, *School-Sanctioned Mid-18th-Century Hazing Rituals at Harvard*, SLATE (Sept. 02, 2014, 9:31 A M) , https://slate.com/human-interest/2014/09/history-of-harv ard-customs-hazing-rituals-of-the-school-in-the-18th-centu ry.html.

- Phil Cross, *Toxic Traditions? Alleged Sexual Assault, Violence Creeps Way Into Team Hazing Rituals*, FOX 25 (Oct. 26th 2018, 11:25 PM), https://okcfox.com/news/local/toxic-traditions-alle ged-sexual-assault-violence-creep-into-team-hazing-rituals.

- Connor Simpson, *What Hazing Is Like at the Deadliest Frat*, The Atlantic (Dec. 30, 2013), https://www.theatlantic.com/culture/archive/201 3/12/what-hazing-deadliest-frat/356574/.

- Robin Wilkey, *UC Davis Sued For Allegedly Ignoring Abu-*

sive Hazing At University Fraternity, HUFFINGTON POST (Jan 9, 2012), https://www.huffpost.com/entry/uc-davis-s ued-by-ryan-clifford_n_1084769.

- David Boroff, *TCU Fraternity Shut Down in Wake of Hazing Allegations After Members Were Told to Perform With Sex Toys*, NEW YORK DAILY NEWS (Jan. 5, 2018, 5:09 P   M   )   , https://www.nydailynews.com/2018/01/05/tcu-fraternity -shut-down-in-wake-of-hazing-allegations-after-members-w ere-told-to-perform-with-sex-toys/.

- Jill Harmacinski, *Andover Hazing Detailed in Lawsuit*, THE EAGLE   TRIBUNE   (Jan.   8,   2018), https://www.eagletribune.com/news/andover-hazing-detail ed-in-lawsuit/article_e7796610-36a1-578c-b397-4216bcfc ded7.html.

- Jason Silverstein, *Texas High School Ignored 'Sadistic' Sexual Hazing Rituals on Sports Teams, Suit Says*, NEW YORK DAILY NEWS (Apr. 12, 2017, 9:53 AM), https://www.nydailynews.com/2017/04/12/texas-high-sch ool-ignored-sadistic-sexual-hazing-rituals-on-sports-teams-s uit-says/.

- Kevin Lewis, *'The Hazing Ritual is Notorious.' Damascus H.S. Rape Victims File Lawsuit Against MCPS*, ABC 7 (Feb. 6th   2020,   10:34   AM), https://wjla.com/news/local/damascus-hs-sex-assault-victi ms-file-civil-lawsuit-against-mcps-coaches-administrators.

- *Hazing*, ESPN, https://www.espn.com/espn/feature/story

/_/id/17507010/otl-investigation-trend-sodomy-hazing.

- David K. Li, *Lawsuit Says Penn State Football Players Threatened to 'Sandusky' Teammates in Hazings*, NBC NEWS (Jan. 16, 2020, 10:15 AM), https://www.nbcnews.com/news/us-news/lawsuit-claims -penn-state-football-players-threatened-sandusky-teammate s-hazings-n1115511.

- *Horrifying Violation of Young Athletes*, ABC NEWS (Sept. 30, 2016, 5:10 PM), https://abcnews.go.com/Sports/horr ifying-violation-young-athletes/story?id=42484845.

- Josiah Bates, *Does College Hazing Defy the Laws It Spawned?*, THE MARSHALL PROJECT, https://www.themarshallproject.org/2016/08/21/d oes-college-hazing-defy-the-laws-it-spawned.

- Sheridan Hendrix & Mike Wagner, *So Far, Fraternity Hazing Deaths Haven't Changed Ohio law. Will BGSU, Stone Foltz be Different?*, THE COLUMBUS DISPATCH (Mar. 16, 2021), https://www.dispatch.com/story/news/lo- cal/2021/03/08/bowling-green-hazing-death-ohio-lawmak- ers-could-make-hazing-felony/4626951001/.

  H.R. 3267, 116 Cong. (1st Sess. 2020).

- *Report Details Hazing at Roberton Football Camp*, SANTA FE NEW MEXICAN (Sept. 11, 2008), https://www.santafenewmexican.com/news/local_news/re port-details-hazing-at-robertson-football-camp/article_658

20cbf-ec3b-5948-aad0-f9120d0da7c7.html.

- *Seamons v. Snow*, 84 F..3d 1226, 1230 (10th Cir. 1996).

- *Oncale v. Sundowner Offshore Servs Inc*, 523 U.S. 75, 78, 118 S. Ct. 998, 1001, 140 L. Ed. 2d 201 (1998).

- Jessica Schrader, *Sexual Assault Is About Power*, PSYCHOLOGY TODAY (Nov. 14, 2017), https://www.psychologytoday.com/us/blog/psychoanalysis -unplugged/201711/sexual-assault-is-about-power.

- Joanita Miley, *Traditional Hazing Crosses Line to Sexual Assault*, U.S. ARMY (Dec. 22, 2020), https://www.army.mil/article/242011/traditional_ hazing_crosses_line_to_sexual_assault.

- Dan Lamothe, *Male On Male Sexual Assault in the Military: Overlooked and Hard to Fix, Investigation Finds*, WASHINGTON POST (Mar. 20, 2015), https://www.washingtonpost.com/news/checkpoint/wp/2 015/03/20/male-on-male-sexual-assault-in-the-military-not -addressed-enough-and-hard-to-fix-investigation-finds/

- Nathaniel Penn, *"Son, Men Don't Get Raped"*, GQ (Sept. 2, 2014), https://www.gq.com/story/male-rape-in-the-mili tary.

Why Doesn't She Just Say No?

- Alex Manley, *How to Deal With Rejection the Right Way*, ASK MEN (May 10, 2019), https://www.askmen.com/dating/dating_advice/h

ow-to-handle-rejection-the-right-way.html.

- Suzanne Degges-White, *Romantic Rejection: Why Does It Hurt So Much?*, PSYCHOLOGY TODAY (Jun. 22, 2018), https://www.psychologytoday.com/us/blog/lifetime-conn ections/201806/romantic-rejection-why-does-it-hurt-so-m uch.

- Claire Spellberg, *'Revenge of the Nerds' Filmmakers Address Controversial Rape Scene: "I Regret That"*, DECIDER (Jul. 26, 2019, 10:45 AM), https://decider.com/2019/07/26/reven ge-of-the-nerds-rape-scene-regret/.

- Yael Halon, *Laura Ingraham rips John Legend's 'PC' rewrite of 'Baby, It's Cold Outside'*, FOX NEWS (Nov. 1, 2019, 1:32 P   M   )   , https://www.foxnews.com/media/laura-ingraham-pc-rewri te-of-baby-its-cold-outside-is-historical-and-cultural-terrori sm.

- Sezin Koehler, *From The Mouths of Rapists: The Lyrics of Robin Thicke's 'Blurred Lines'*, PACIFIC STANDARD (Oct. 23, 2018), https://psmag.com/social-justice/mouths-rapist s-lyrics-robin-thickes-blurred-lines-66569.

- RJ Cubarrubia, *Rick Ross Issues Official Apology for 'Rape' Lyrics*, ROLLING STONE (Apr. 12, 2013), https://www.rollingstone.com/music/music-news/ rick-ross-issues-official-apology-for-rape-lyrics-191724/.

- *Stalking Fact Sheet*, STALKING RESOURCE CENTER, https ://www.una.edu/manesafety/Stalking/stalkingfacts.pdf.

- Shaun Nichols, *Ex From Hell Gets Six Years for Online Stalking, Revenge Pics Campaign Against Two Women*, THE REGISTER (Nov. 8, 2019), https://www.theregister.com/2 019/11/08/six_years_cyberstalking_sentence/.

- Robert   T   Muller,   *In   the   Mind   of a   Stalker*, PSYCHOLOGY   TODAY   (Jun.   22, 2013), https://www.psychologytoday.com/us/blog/talkin g-about-trauma/201306/in-the-mind-of-a-stalker.

- Robert P. Burriss, *Why Some Men Respond to Rejection with Aggression*, PSYCHOLOGY TODAY (Mar. 28, 2018), https://www.psychologytoday.com/us/blog/attraction-evo lved/201803/why-some-men-respond-rejection-aggression.

- Sarah Caldwell Hancock, *Psychologist Develops Scale to Measure Masculine Honor Beliefs*, MEDICAL XPRESS (Mar. 1, 2016), https://medicalxpress.com/news/2016-03-psychol ogist-scale-masculine-honor-beliefs.html#google_vignette.

- *Southern California Man Who Ejaculated into Co-Workers Belongings Sentenced to 2 1/2 Years in Jail*, CBS 8 (Oct. 14, 2   0   2   0   )   , https://www.cbs8.com/article/news/crime/southern-califor nia-man-ejaculated-semen-co-workers-belongings-sentence d-jail-sex-offender-stevens-millancastro/509-f8cae58c-9847 -4ddb-b157-097c230e35bf.

- Zeba Blay, *Tiarah Poyau's Murder Exposes The Black Male Fragility We Don't Talk About*, HUFFINGTON POST (Sep 8, 2016,   05:17   PM), https://www.huffpost.com/entry/tiarah-poyaus-murder-ex

poses-the-black-male-fragility-we-dont-talk-about_n_57d1
751be4b00642712bd58a.

* Sasha Goldstein, *Engaged Mom-of-3 Shot Dead After Snubbing Man at Detroit Bar, Family Says*, NEW YORK DAILY NEWS (Oct. 7, 2014, 4:32 PM), https://www.nydailynews.com/2014/10/07/engaged-mom -of-3-shot-dead-after-snubbing-man-at-detroit-bar-family-s ays/.

* Clementine Ford, *When Male Entitlement Meets Rejection*, DAILY LIFE (May 27, 2016), http://www.dailylife.com.au/news-and-views/dl-opinion/ when-male-entitlement-meets-rejection-20160526-gp501q. html.

* *Men's Violent Reactions to Women's Rejection*, MEDICAL XPRESS, Dec. 4, 2014), https://medicalxpress.com/news/ 2014-12-men-violent-reactions-women.html.

* Siwaphiwe Myataza, *Raising Men to Handle Romantic Rejection can Diminish Violence Against Women*, MAIL AND GUARDIAN (Jun. 25, 2020), https://mg.co.za/thought-leader/opinion/2020-06-25-raisi ng-men-to-handle-romantic-rejection-can-diminish-violenc e-against-women/.

(Non-Consensual) Sex on the Beach: Bystander Theory
* Victims of Sexual Violence: Statistics, RAINN, https://w ww.rainn.org/statistics/victims-sexual-violence.

- Elly Belle, *Bystander Intervention Can Stop Sexual Assault Before it Happens*, Teen Vogue (Apr. 4, 2018), https://www.teenvogue.com/story/bystander-intervention-guide-sexual-assault.

- Edecio Martinez, *Richmond High School Gang-Rape in California: Others Watched and Did Nothing, Say Cops*, CBS News (Oct. 27, 2009, 8:28 AM), https://www.cbsnews.com/news/richmond-high-school-gang-rape-in-california-others-watched-and-did-nothing-say-cops/.

- *Bystander Effect*, Psychology Today, https://www.psychologytoday.com/us/basics/bystander-effect.

- Kendra Cherry, *How Psychology Explains the Bystander Effect*, Very Well Mind (June 07, 2023), https://www.verywellmind.com/the-bystander-effect-2795899.

- *Gang Rape Witnesses Kept Silent So They Wouldn't Be Called Snitches*, ABC News (Nov. 11, 2009, 11:56 AM), https://abcnews.go.com/WN/Health/witnesses-california-gang-rape-scared-call-police/story?id=9054150.

- Don Palmerine, *I Watched a Rape. For Five Decades, I Did Nothing*, Washington Post (Oct. 5, 2018, 10:56 AM), https://www.washingtonpost.com/outlook/i-watched-a-rape-for-five-decades-i-did-nothing/2018/10/05/f28d9cf8-c805-11e8-b2b5-79270f9cce17_story.html.

- *Margaret W. v.. Kelly R.*, 139 Cal. App. 4th 141, 149, 42 Cal. Rptr. 3d 519, 525 (2006).

- *M.W. v. Panama Buena Vista Union Sch. Dist.*, 110 Cal. App, 4th 508, 511, 1 Cal. Rpt. 3d 673, 675 (2003).

- *Witnesses: We Broke Up Gang Rape of Girl, 17*, ABC News (Jun. 3, 2009, 3:08 PM), https://abcnews.go.com/2020/st ory?id=7748009&page=1.

  Kristin Wright, *Homeless Man Stops Rape Attempt in Northwest D.C.*, NBC 4 (Mar. 27, 2015, 10:37 PM), https://www.nbcwashington.com/news/local/home less-man-stops-rape-attempt-in-northwest-dc/63501/.

- Amanda Taub, *The Vanderbilt Trial Shows Why Bystanders Have No Incentive to Stop Rape*, Vox (Feb 2, 2015, 12:30 PM), https://www.vox.com/2015/2/2/7963277/vanderbi lt-rape-culture.

- Michael Winerip, *Stepping Up to Stop Sexual Assault*, New York Times (Feb. 7, 2014), https://www.nytimes.com/2014/02/09/education/ edlife/stepping-up-to-stop-sexual-assault.html.

When We Cry

- Jenna Lemoncelli, *Stephen A. Smith rants on Will Smith's Oscars smack: 'Straight bulls–t'*, NY Post (Mar. 28, 2022), https://nypost.com/2022/03/28/stephen-a-smi th-calls-will-smiths-chris-rock-smack-bulls-t/.

- Audrey Nelson, *Why Don't Many Men Show Their Emotions?*, Psychology Today (Jan. 24, 2015), https://www.psychologytoday.com/us/blog/he-speaks-she

-speaks/201501/why-don-t-many-men-show-their-emotion
s.

- Miranda Perez, *"Man Up!": Why Men Of Color Don't Cry*, HER CAMPUS (Oct 9, 2017), https://www.hercampus.co m/school/cau/man-why-men-color-dont-cry/.

- Candice Ortiz, *Charlamagne Says Chris Rock's Joke is a 'Very Small Part' of Will Smith's Problems: 'There is Something Way Deeper Going On'*, MEDIAITE (Mar 28th, 2022, 1:02 P   M   )   , https://www.mediaite.com/podcasts/charlamagne-says-chri s-rocks-joke-is-a-very-small-part-of-will-smiths-problems-th ere-is-something-way-deeper-going-on/.

- *'No Way Out?' Black Male Suicides Rising Faster Than Any Other Racial Group*, THE OBSERVER (Feb. 15, 2022), https://sacobserver.com/2022/02/no-way-out-black-male-s uicides-rising-faster-than-any-other-racial-group/?msclkid= b1f8642db1dc11ec92b249d500a91ff4.

- Jamilah Pitts, *The Black Church Cannot 'Pray Away' Mental Illness*, HUFFINGTON POST (Aug 29, 2018, 12:04 PM), https://www.huffpost.com/entry/opinion-black-church-th erapy_n_5b86957ee4b0162f471e398d?msclkid=d94af213 b1e211ecbd9e738e11d50dff.

- Kynala Phillips, *Chance the Rapper Unpacks Why Black Men Are 'So Guarded' About Their Emotions*, NBC NEWS (Nov. 2, 2021, 4:09 PM), https://www.nbcnews.com/news/nbcblk/chance-ra pper-unpacks-black-men-are-guarded-emotions-rcna4336.

- Rebecca Morris, *Just What Does it Take to Make Someone Snap?*, SEATTLE TIMES (Feb. 15, 2007, 12:00 AM), https://www.seattletimes.com/life/lifestyle/just-what-does-it-take-to-make-someone-snap/?msclkid=10d4cb47b1cc1 1ecba38d46f18eb35d4.

- *What Can Cause Someone to Snap?*, ABC NEWS (Oct. 3, 2006, 3:44 PM), https://abcnews.go.com/Health/story?id=2522873&page=1&msclkid=3330510ab12c11ecb72132af80fcb208.

- Elle Kwan, *A Teacher's Kind Response to Toddler Crying at School Inspires Parent*, HAND IN HAND, https://www.handinhandparenting.org/2017/01/toddler-crying-at-school/.

The Monster at My Law School

- Child Pornography, The United States Department of Justice, https://www.justice.gov/criminal-ceos/child-pornography.

- Protection of Children Against Sexual Exploitation Act, Pub. L. No. 95-225.S.1585,95th Cong. (1978).

- H.R. 5210, 100th Cong. (1988).

- S.3266, 101st. Cong. (1990).

- Tom Vanden Brook, *Air Force Colonel Slated to Command Base That Hosts Air Force One is Sentenced in, Child Porn Case*, USA TODAY (Feb. 3, 2020, 11:26 AM), https://www.usatoday.com/story/news/politics/2020/02/03/air-force-colonel-slated-to-command-base-that-hosts-air-f orce-one-is-sentenced-in-child-porn/4646319002/.

• *Kansas Priest Sentenced to Prison for Possessing Child Porn*, U.S. NEWS & WORLD REPORT (Jul. 15, 2020, 5:16 PM), https//www.usanews.com/news/best-states/kansas/articles /2020-07-15/kansas-priest-sentenced-to-prison-for-possessi ng-child-porn.

• Andrew Denney, et. al., *Feds Found 'Vast Trove' of Nude Photos in Jeffery Epstien's Safe*, NEW YORK POST (Jul. 8, 2019, 9:17 PM), https://nypost.com/2019/07/08/feds-fo und-vast-trove-of-nude-photos-in-jeffery-epstiens-safe/.

• Nick Bogert & Erik Ortiz, Jared Fogle, *Ex- Subway Pitchman, Gets 15 Years in Prison for Child Porn Charges*, NBC NEWS (Nov. 19, 2015, 10:49 AM), https://www.nbcnews.com/news/us-news/jared-fogle-ex-s ubway-pitchman-pleads-guilty-child-porn-sex-n466256.

• Michael H. Kelly & Gabriel J.X. Dance, *The Internet Is Overrun With Images of Child Sexual Abuse. What Went Wrong?*, NEW YORK TIMES (Sept. 28, 2019), https://nyti mes.com/interactive/2019/09/28/us/child-sex-abuse.html.

• Rae Hodge, *Tor Browser FAQ: What is it and How Does it Protect Your Privacy?*, CNET (Feb. 1, 2021, 6:00 AM), https://www.cnet.com/how-to/tor-browser-faq-wh at-is-it-and-how-does-it-protect-your-privacy/.

• *The Source of Child Pornography*, FBI (Apr. 25, 2017), https://www.fbi.gov/news/stories/the-scourge-of-c hild-pornography.

- *National Strategy for Child Exploitation Prevention and Interdiction*, THE UNITED STATES DEPARTMENT OF JUSTICE, https://www.justice.gov/psc/national-strategy-child-exploitation-prevention-and-interdiction.

- Clark Mindock, *More Than 300 Arrested in Worldwide Sting of 'Largest Dark Web Child Sex Abuse Marketplace Run by Bitcoin'*, INDEPENDENT (Oct. 16, 2019), https://www.independent.co.uk/news/world/americas/child-porn-nitcoin-arrests-us-jong-woo-son-a9159146.html.

- Bryan Menegus, *Tumblr Disappeared from the App Store Because of Child Porn*, GIZMODO (Nov. 19, 2018, 10:00 PM), https:/gizmodo.com/tumblr-disappeared-from-the-app-store-because-of-child-1830553237.

- *Kik Statement to "48 Hours'*, CBS NEWS (Jun. 3, 2017), https://www.cbsnews.com/news/kik-app-statement-to-48-hours-may-2017/.

- *Raleigh Man Who is a Convicted Sex Offender Sentenced to 20 Years for the Receipt of Child Pornography*, THE UNITED STATES ATTORNEY'S OFFICE EASTERN DISTRICT OF NORTH CAROLINA (Oct. 10, 2017), https://www.justice.gov/usao-ednc/pr/raleigh-man-who-convicted-sex-offender-sentenced-20-years-receipt-child-pornography.

- *California Man Sentences to 14 Years in Prison for Sexually Exploiting a Minor He Met While Playing "Clash of Clans"*, THE UNITED STATES DEPARTMENT OF JUSTICE (May 31, 2 0 1 9) ,

https://www.justice.gov/opa/pr/california-man-sentenced
-14-years-prison-sexually-exploiting-minor-he-met-while-pl
aying-clash.

- *Accused Child Predator Used 'Fortnite' to Lure Teen into Sexual Relationship, Deputies Say*, NBC 12 (Jan. 20, 2019, 1:21   AM), https://www.nbc12.com/2019/01/20/accused-child-preda tor-used-fortnite-to-lure-teen-into-sexual-relationship-depu ties-say/.

- Olivia Solon, *Child Sexual Abuse Images and Online Exploitation Surge During Pandemic*, NBC NEWS (Apr. 23, 2020,   3:01   PM), https://www.nbcnews.com/tech/tech-news/child-sexual-a buse-images-online-exploitation-surge-during-pandemic-n1 190506.

- Pete Yost, *DOJ: Operation Delego Targets International Child Porn Network*, POLICE 1 (Aug. 3, 2011), https://www.police1.com/federal-law-enforcement/articles /doj-operation-delego-targets-international-child-porn-net work-QyeO8QIsPpqdgZP0/.

- *Operation Predator- Targeting Child Exploitation and Sexual Crimes*, U.S. IMMIGRATION AND CUSTOMS ENFORCE-MENT (Jun. 25, 2012), https://www.ice.gov/factsheets/pre dator.

- *Compulsive   Sexual   Behavior*, MAYO   CLIN-IC, https://www.mayoclinic.org/diseases-conditions/comp ulsive-sexual-behavior/symptoms-causes/syc-20360434.

- Adam Felman, *What to Know About Compulsive Sexual Behavior*, MEDICAL NEWS TODAY (Oct. 8, 2019), https://m edicalnewstoday.com/articles/182473.

- Samantha Smithstein, *Who's Looking at Child Porn Now (and Why?)*, PSYCHOLOGY TODAY (May 30, 2017), https://www.psychologytoday.com/us/blog/what-the-wild -things-are/201009/whos-looking-child-porn-now-and-wh y.

- Karen Franklin, *Why Are These Men Downloading Child Pornography*, PSYCHOLOGY TODAY (May 30, 2017), https://www.psychologytoday.com/us/blog/witness/2017 05/why-are-these-men-downloading-child-pornography.

- Anna Borgstrom, *The Myth of the Harmless Hands-Off Offender*, NET CLEAN (Apr. 27, 2017), https://www.netclean.com/2017/04/27/the-myth -of-the-harmless-hands-off-offender/.

- Bourke, M.L., Hernandez, A.E. The 'Butner Study' Redux: A Report of the Incidence of Hands-on Child Victimization by Child Pornography Offenders. *J Fam Viol* 24, 183 (2009). https://doi.org/10.1007/s10896-008-9219-y.

- Seto MC, Karl Hanson R, Babchishin KM. Contact Sexual Offending by Men With Online Sexual Offenses. *Sexual Abuse*. 2011;23(1):124-145. doi:10.1177/1079063210369 013.

- *Contributing Factors to Child Abuse and Neglect*, Children's Wisconsin, https://childrenswi.org.

- Elizabeth Hartney, *The Cycle of Sexual Abuse and Abusive Adult Relationships*, VERY WELL MIND (May 4, 2019), https://www.verywellmind.com/the-cycle-of-sexual-abuse-22460.

ABOUT THE AUTHOR

James Wilkerson is a native of New Albany, Indiana. He holds his Masters degree in communication from Bellarmine University and his Bachelors degree and Juris Doctorate from the University of Louisville. In 2016, he founded Greek Law; a program that allowed him to give lectures on sexual assault prevention and consent at various fraternity and sorority chapters around the country. Wilkerson is a TedX speaker, having presented lectures at TEDxBloomington (2021), TEDxBellarmine (2022), and TEDxLSSU (2023). He was named one of Louisville Business First's "20 People You Should Know in Law" in 2019 and was inducted into their "40 Under 40" class of 2021. He is a three-time winner of the Louisville Eccentric Observer's Best Local Writer Award (2021, 2022, 2023). He currently teaches gender studies at Indiana University Southeast, as well as his flagship course, Advanced Issues in Criminal Law: Sex Offenses at his alma mater, the University of Louisville Brandeis School of Law.